OSAMA'S REVENGE

ADVANCE PRAISE FOR *OSAMA'S REVENGE*

"Finally! An authoritative work that details the 'dirty secret' which no one until now has analyzed: the uninterrupted connection between the international drug trade and global terrorist networks. Paul Williams has provided tremendous insight into some of the most critical issues confronting the United States today. A must-read for all Americans!"

—Andrew R. Thomas
security analyst and author of *Aviation Insecurity* and *Air Rage*

"Dr. Paul Williams's brilliant treatise on terrorism factually establishes bin Laden's modus operandi, which America's leadership would just as soon not see raised; that bin Laden became empowered as a master terrorist by American foreign policy and his Jihad massively financed by American drug consumption. Small wonder, as Williams points out, that bin Laden dismisses Americans as 'self-destructive.'"

—Mitchell Grochowski
Managing Editor, the *Guard*

"Williams is a master of research and getting his facts straight. He takes the reader into the world of the Chechen Mafia and exposes its connection to Osama bin Laden's al Qaeda. A must-read, to fully understand the imminent threat of terrorism."

—Peter James Killeen
host of *The Police Connection* radio show

"A fascinating and frightening look at the threat of terrorism. . . . A must-read for every concerned American."

—Dan Gulbin
Associate Editor, the *Metro*
Scranton, Pennsylvania

OSAMA'S REVENGE

THE NEXT 9/11

What the Media and the
Government Haven't Told You

PAUL L. WILLIAMS

Prometheus Books

59 John Glenn Drive
Amherst, New York 14228-2197

Published 2004 by Prometheus Books

Inquiries should be addressed to
Prometheus Books
59 John Glenn Drive
Amherst, New York 14228–2197
VOICE: 716–691–0133, ext. 207
FAX: 716–564–2711
WWW.PROMETHEUSBOOKS.COM

08 07 06 05 04   5 4 3 2 1

Library of Congress Cataloging-in-Publication Data

Williams, Paul L., 1944–
    Osama's revenge : the next 9-11 / Paul L. Williams.
        p. cm.
    Includes bibliographical references and index.
    ISBN 1–59102–252–5 (hardcover : alk. paper)
    1. Qaida (Organization). 2. Terrorism—United States—Forecasting. 3. Nuclear terrorism—United States—Forecasting. I. Title.

HV6432.5.Q2W55 2004
303.6'25'0973—dc22

                                                                        2004006986

Printed in Canada on acid-free paper

For Katherine Delores Williams,
my hope for the future

CONTENTS

CONTENTS

A LETTER TO AMERICA

by Osama bin Laden

Some American writers have published articles under the title "On What Basis Are We Fighting?" These articles have generated a number of responses, some of which adhered to the truth and were based on Islamic Law, and others that were not. Here we wanted to outline the truth—as an explanation and warning—hoping for Allah's reward, seeking success and support from Him.

While seeking Allah's help, we form our reply on two questions directed at the Americans:

Why are we fighting and opposing you?

What are we calling you to, and what do we want from you?

As for the first question: Why are we fighting and opposing you? The answer is very simple: Because you attacked us and continue to attack us.

You attacked us in Palestine, which has sunk under military occupation for more than eighty years. The British handed over Palestine with your help and your support to the Jews, who have occupied it for more than fifty years; years overflowing with oppression, tyranny, crimes, killings, expulsions, destruction and devastation. The creation and continuation of Israel is one of the greatest crimes, and you are the leader of its criminals. And, of course, there is no need to explain and prove the degree of American support for Israel. The creation of Israel is a crime that must be erased. Each and every person whose hands have become polluted in the contribution towards this crime must pay its price and pay it heavily.

It brings us both laughter and tears to see that you have not yet tired of repeating your fabricated lies that the Jews have a historical right to Palestine, as it was promised to them in the Torah. Anyone who disputes with you or them on this alleged fact is accused of Anti-Semitism. This is one of the most fallacious, widely circulated fabrications in history. The people of Palestine are pure Arabs and original Semites. It is the Muslims who are the inheritors of Moses (peace be unto him) and the inheritors of the real Torah that has not been changed. Muslims believe in all the prophets, including Abraham, Moses, Jesus and Muhammad (peace and blessings of Allah be upon them all). If the followers of Moses have been promised a right to Palestine, then the Muslims are the most worthy nation of this. . . .

You attacked us in Somalia; you supported the Russian atrocities against us in Chechnya; the Indian oppression against us in Kashmir; and the Jewish aggression against us in Lebanon. Under your supervision, consent and orders, the governments of these countries attack us on a daily basis. . . .

You steal our wealth and oil at paltry prices because of your international influence and military threats. This theft is, indeed, the biggest theft ever witnessed by mankind in the history of the world.

Your forces occupy our countries; you spread your military bases throughout them; you corrupt our lands; and you besiege our sanctities to protect the security of the Jews and to ensure the continuity of your pillage of our treasures.

You have starved the Muslims of Iraq, where children die every day. It is a wonder that more than 1.5 million Iraqi children have died as a result of your sanctions, and you did not show concern. Yet when three thousand of your people died, the entire world rises and has not yet sat down.

You have supported the Jews in their idea that Jerusalem is their eternal capital and you have agreed to move your embassy there. With your help and under your protection, the Israelis are planning to destroy the Al-Aqsa mosque. Under the protection of your weapons, Sharon entered the Al-Aqsa mosque to pollute it as a preparation to capture and destroy it.

These tragedies and calamities are only a few examples of your oppression and aggression against us. It is commanded by our religion and intellect that the oppressed have a right to return the aggression. Do not await anything from us except *jihad*, resistance, and revenge. Is it in any way rational to expect that after America has attacked us for more than half a century, that we will then leave her to live in security and peace???

You may dispute that all of the above does not justify aggression against civilians for crimes they did not commit and offenses in which they did not partake. This argument contradicts your continuous repetition that America is the land of freedom and its leaders in this world. For this reason, the American people are the ones who choose their government by way of their own free will: a choice that stems from their agreement to its policies. Thus the American people have chosen, consented to, and affirmed their support for the Israeli oppression of the Palestinians, the occupation and usurpation of Palestinian lands, and the continuous killing, torture, punishment and expulsion of the Palestinian people. The American people have the ability and choice to reject the policies of their government and even to change it if they want.

The American people are the ones who pay the taxes that fund the planes that bomb us in Afghanistan, the tanks that strike and destroy our homes in Palestine, the armies that occupy our lands in the Arabian Gulf, and the fleets that ensure the blockade of Iraq. These tax dollars are given to Israel for it to continue to attack us and penetrate our lands. In this way, the American people remain the ones who fund the attacks against us, and they are the ones who oversee the expenditure of these monies in the way they wish through their elected candidates. Also, the American army is part of the American people. It is these very same people who are shamelessly helping the Jews fight against us. The American people are the ones who employ both their men and women in the American forces that attack us. This is why the American people cannot be innocent of all the crimes committed by the Americans and the Jews against us.

Allah, the Almighty, legislated the permission and the option to take revenge. Thus, if we are attacked, then we have the right to attack back. When they destroy our villages and towns, then we have the right to destroy their villages and towns. If they steal our wealth, then we have the right to destroy their economy. And when they kill our civilians, then we have the right to kill theirs.

As for the second question that we want to answer: What are we calling you to and what do we want from you?

The first thing that we are calling you to is Islam: the religion of the Unification of God; of freedom from associating partners with him, and complete rejection of this; of complete love of Him, the Exalted; of complete submission to His laws; and of the discarding of all the opinions, orders, theories and religions that contradict with this religion. He sent down His Prophet Muhammad (peace be unto him). Islam is the religion of all the prophets and makes no distinction between them (peace be unto them all).

It is to this religion that we call you: the seal of all the previous religions. It is the religion of unification of God, sincerity, the best of manners, righteousness, mercy, honor, purity and piety. It is the religion of showing kindness to others, establishing justice between them, granting them their rights, and defending the oppressed and the persecuted. It is the religion of enjoining the good and forbidding the evil with the hand, tongue and heart. It is the religion of *jihad* in the way of Allah so that Allah's word and religion reign supreme. And it is the religion of unity and agreement on the obedience to Allah, and total equality between all people, without regarding their color, sex or language.

It is the religion whose book—the Koran—will remain preserved and unchanged, after the other divine books and messages have been changed. The Koran is the miracle until the Day of Judgment. Allah has challenged anyone to bring forth a book like the Koran or even ten verses like it.

The second thing to which we call you is a demand to stop your oppression, lies, immorality, and debauchery that have spread among you. We call you to be a people of manners, principles, honor and purity and to reject the immoral acts of fornication, homosexuality, intoxicants, gambling, and trading with interest. We call you to all this that you may be freed from that in which you have become enmeshed; that you may be freed from the deceptive lies that you are a great nation—lies that your leaders spread among you to conceal from you the despicable state to which you have descended.

It is saddening to tell you that you are the worst civilization witnessed by the history of mankind. You are a nation who, rather than ruling by the *shariah* of Allah in its Constitution and Laws, choose to invent your own laws as you will and desire. You separate religion from your policies, contradicting the pure nature that affirms Absolute Authority to the Lord and your Creator. . . .

You are the nation that permits Usury that has been forbidden by all the religions. Yet you build your economy and investments on Usury. As a result of this, in all its different forms and guises, the Jews have taken control of your economy, through which they have then taken control of your media, and all aspects of your life, making you their servants and achieving their aims at your expense: precisely what Benjamin Franklin warned you against.

You are a nation that permits the production, trading and usage of intoxicants. You also permit drugs, and only forbid the trade of them, even though your nation is the largest consumer of them.

You are a nation that permits acts of immorality, and you consider them to be pillars of personal freedom. You have continued to sink down this abyss from level to level until incest has spread among you, in the face of which neither your sense of honor nor your laws object. Who can forget your President Clinton's immoral acts committed in the official Oval Office? After that you did not even bring him to account, other than that he "made a mistake," after which everything passed with no punishment. Is there a worse kind of event for which your name will go down in history and be remembered by nations?

You are a nation that permits gambling in all its forms. The companies practice this as well, resulting in the investments becoming active and the criminals becoming rich.

You are a nation that exploits women like consumer products or advertising tools, calling upon customers to purchase them. You use women to serve passengers, visitors and strangers to increase your profit margins. You then rant that you support the liberation of women.

You are a nation that practices the trade of sex in all its forms, directly or indirectly. Giant corporations and establishments are based on this, under the name of art, entertainment, tourism and freedom, and other deceptive names you attribute to it.

And because of all this, you have been described in history as a nation that spreads diseases that were unknown to man in the past. Go ahead and boast to the nations of man that you brought them AIDS as a Satanic American invention.

You have destroyed nature with your industrial waste and gases more than any other nation in history. Despite this, you refuse to sign the Kyoto agreement so that you can secure the profit of your greedy companies and industries.

Your law is the law of the rich and wealthy people, who hold sway in their political parties, and fund their election campaign with their gifts. Behind them stand the Jews, who control your policies, media and economy.

That which you are singled out for in the history of mankind, is that you have used your force to destroy mankind more than any other nation in history; not to defend principles and values, but to hasten to secure your interests and profits. You dropped a nuclear bomb on Japan, even though Japan was ready to negotiate an end to the war!!! How many acts of oppression, tyranny and injustice have you carried out, O callers to freedom?

Let us not forget one of your major characteristics: your duality in both manners and values; your hypocrisy in manners and principles. All manners, principles and values have two scales: one for you and one for the others.

The freedom and democracy that you espouse is for yourselves and for the white race only; as for the rest of the world, you impose upon them your monstrous, destructive policies and governments that you call your "American friends." Yet you prevent them from establishing democracies. When the Islamic party in Algeria wanted to practice democracy and they won the election, you unleashed your agents in the Algerian army onto them to attack them with tanks and guns to imprison them and torture them—a new lesson from the "American book of democracy."

Your policy on prohibiting and forcibly removing weapons of

mass destruction to ensure world peace: it only applies to those countries that you do not permit to possess such weapons. As for the countries you consent to, such as Israel, then they are allowed to keep and use such weapons to defend their security. Anyone else whom you suspect might be manufacturing or keeping these kinds of weapons, you call them criminals and you take military action against them.

You are the last ones to respect the resolutions and policies of international law, yet you claim to want to selectively punish anyone else who does the same. Israel has for more than fifty years been pushing UN resolutions and rules against the wall with the full support of America.

As for war criminals that you censure and for whom you form criminal court, you shamelessly ask that your own war criminals be granted immunity! However, history will not forget the war crimes that you committed against the Muslims and the rest of the world; those you have killed in Japan, Afghanistan, Somalia, Lebanon and Iraq. These crimes will remain a shame that you will never be able to escape. It will suffice to remind you of your latest war crimes in Afghanistan, in which densely populated innocent civilian villages were destroyed and bombs were dropped on mosques, causing the roof of the mosque to come crashing down on the heads of Muslims praying inside. You are the ones who broke the agreement with the *mujahadeen* when they left Qunduz, bombing them in Janqi fort and killing more than one thousand of your prisoners through suffocation and thirst. Allah alone knows how many people have died by torture at your hands and the hands of your agents. Your planes remain in the Afghan skies, looking for anyone remotely suspicious.

You have claimed to be the vanguards of human rights and your Ministry of Foreign Affairs issues annual reports containing the statistics of those countries that violate any human rights. However, all these things vanished when the *mujahadeen* hit you. You then implemented the methods of the same documented governments that you used to curse. In America, you captured thousands of Muslims and Arabs and took them into custody with neither reason nor court trial nor even disclosing the names. You issued newer, harsher laws. What happened in Guantanamo is a historical embarrassment to America and its values. It screams in your faces. You hypocrites, what is the value of your signature on any agreement or treaty?

Thirdly, we call you to take an honest stance with yourselves—and I doubt you will do so—to discover that you are a nation without principles or values, and that the values and principles to you are something that your merely demand from others—not that to which you yourself must adhere.

Fourthly, we call you to stop supporting Israel; to stop your support of the Indians in Kashmir and the Russians against the Chechens; and to stop your support of the Manila government against the Muslims in the southern Philippines.

Fifthly, we call you to pack your luggage and get out of our lands. We desire for the sake of goodness, guidance and righteousness that you do not force us to send you back as cargo in coffins.

Sixthly, we call upon you to end your support of the corrupt leaders in our countries. Do not interfere in our politics and methods of education. Leave us alone, or else expect us in New York and Washington.

Finally, we call upon you to deal with us and interact with us on the basis of mutual interests and benefits, rather than the policies of subjugation, theft and occupation, and not to continue your policy of supporting the Jews because this will result in more disasters for you.

If you fail to respond to all these conditions, then prepare for war with the Islamic Nation—the Nation of Monotheism that puts complete trust in Allah and fears none other than him—the Nation that is addressed by the Koran with these words: "Do you fear them? Allah has more right that you should fear Him if you are believers. Fight against them so that Allah will punish them by your hands and disgrace them and give you victory over them and heal the breasts of the believing people and remove the anger from their hearts. Allah accepts the repentance of whom He wills. Allah is all knowing and all wise" (Koran 9:13–14).

The Islamic Nation is the Nation of Honor and Respect: "But honor, power and glory to Allah, and to his Messenger (peace be unto him) and to the believers" (Koran 63:8); "So do not become weak (against your enemy), nor be sad, and you will be superior (in victory), if you are indeed believers" (Koran 3:139).

The Islamic Nation is the Nation of Martyrdom, the Nation that desires death more than you desire life: "Think not of those who are killed in the way of Allah as dead. Nay, they are alive with their Lord, and they are being provided for. They rejoice in what Allah has bestowed upon them from his bounty and rejoice for the sake of those who have not yet joined them, but are left behind (not yet martyred) that no fear will come upon them and that they will not grieve. They rejoice in a grace and a bounty from Allah, and that Allah will not waste the reward of the believers" (Koran 3:169–71).

The Islamic Nation is the Nation of Victory and Success that Allah has promised: "It is he who has sent his Messenger (Muhammad, peace be unto him) with guidance and the religion of truth (Islam) to make it victorious over all other religions, even though the polytheists hate it" (Koran 61:9); "Allah has decreed, 'Verily, it is I and my Messengers who shall be victorious.' Verily, Allah is all-powerful, all-mighty" (Koran 58:21).

The Islamic Nation that was able to dismiss and destroy the previous evil empires like yourself—the Nation that rejects your attacks—wishes to remove your evils and is prepared to fight you. You are well aware that the Islamic Nation, from the very core of its being, despises your haughtiness and arrogance.

If the Americans refuse to listen to our advice and the goodness, guidance and righteousness to which we call them, then be aware that you will lose this Crusade that Bush began, just like the other previous Crusades in which you were humiliated by the hands of the *mujahadeen*, fleeing to your homes in great silence and disgrace. If the Americans do not respond, then their fate will be that of the Soviets who fled from Afghanistan to deal with their military defeat, political breakup, ideological downfall and economic bankruptcy.

This is our message to the Americans, as an answer to their questions. Do they now know why we fight them and over which form of ignorance, by the permission of Allah, we shall be victorious?

November 24, 2002

PART ONE

DRAINING THE SWAMP

We know that Islam is fully compatible with liberty and tolerance and progress because we see the proof in your country and in our own.

—President George W. Bush to
President Megawati Sukarno of Jakarta,
October 22, 2003

Are we winning or losing the global war on terror? . . . We are having mixed results with al Qaeda, although we put considerable pressure on them—nonetheless, a great many remain at large. . . . Today we lack metrics to know if we are winning or losing the global war on terror. Are we capturing, killing or deterring and dissuading more terrorists every day than the madrassahs and the radical clerics are recruiting, training and deploying against us? Does the US need to fashion a broad, integrated plan to stop the next generation of terrorists? The US is putting relatively little effort into a long-range plan, but we are putting a great deal of effort into trying to stop terrorists. The cost-benefit ratio is against us. Our cost is billions against the terrorists' cost of millions.

—Memo of Defense Secretary Donald Rumsfeld
to Gen. Dick Myers, Paul Wolfowitz,
Gen. Pete Pace, and Doug Feith, October 16, 2003

CHAPTER 1

THE DRUG CONNECTION

Al Qaeda and the Taliban

We are making these drugs for Satan—America and the Jews. If we cannot kill them with guns so we will kill them with drugs.
—Fatwa of Hezbollah

What better way to poison the West than through drugs. It's another weapon in their arsenal.
—Donnie Marshall, former head of the
US Drug Enforcement Administration

The Afghans are selling 7 to 8 billion dollars of drugs in the West a year. Bin Laden oversees the export of drugs from Afghanistan. His people are involved in growing the crops, processing and shipping. When Americans buy drugs, they fund the jihad.
—Yosef Bodansky, director of the Congressional Task
Force on Terrorism and Unconventional Warfare, 1998

"This stuff is the ultimate. I shot up last night and it kept me so high that I could survey everything. I was above everything—like a transcendent being. I could read Hegel and Heidegger without cracking a yawn. I could solve problems in advanced calculus or quantum physics like Alfred Lord White-head. It's the best shit on the street."

The heroin, measuring a tenth of a gram, comes in a small cellophane packet that is sealed by an adhesive label. The label bears a brand name and an advertising logo. Unlike the old "nickel" and "dime" bags of hash and grass, this stuff has been carefully packaged for mass consumption like old-fashioned penny candy.

The student, sitting across the table at the White Dog Tavern, attends the University of Pennsylvania. He looks fashionably grungy in a soiled sweatshirt and faded jeans. His hair is brown, long, and matted; his face unshaved; and his blue eyes are bloodshot. He is neither a seller nor a pusher. And he doesn't need money. He comes from an upscale family in Saddlebrook, New Jersey. His father manufactures an exclusive line of sporting goods.

"It's a Binny, man," the student says. "You might have sniffed or snorted some horse before, but you've never had anything like this. Try it, man. It's only a hundred a hit and it will take you anyplace you want to go."

The brand name is "bin Laden" and the advertising logo is a crescent moon, the traditional symbol of Islam.[1] Throughout the country, millions of "Binnys" are sold on college campuses and street corners, in professional office buildings and public restrooms, at rock concerts and movie complexes by thousands of drug dealers. The cost fluctuates wildly, ranging from twenty dollars a bag in New York City to two hundred dollars in Pittsburgh. Most customers prefer to make purchases by the "bundle." Each bundle contains ten packs, enough for one month of "recreational" use.

The users aren't particularly concerned that they are funding the *jihad* and the next terrorist attack on America by their purchases. When I mention this to the student, he shrugs his shoulders and says: "Who the hell cares? *Que sera, sera,* man."

24

The Binnys remain the secret behind bin Laden's billions—not his inheritance from his father's massive construction company nor the gifts from wealthy Saudis. The billions came not from investments in shipping lines, manufacturing plants, and Arabian oil companies but rather from an alliance that bin Laden made in Afghanistan with a ragtag Pakistani army called the Taliban.

The Taliban was formed by Mullah Mohammed Omar, a Pashtun veteran and hero of the ten-year *jihad* against the Soviet Union. In one battle at Singesar, about thirty miles west of Kandahar, Omar was blinded in his left eye by a piece of shrapnel. Knowing that his eye was lost and that it could become infected, he ripped the eyeball from its socket, wiped his bloody hand on the wall of a mosque in Singesar, and returned to take part in the engagement with his trusty Kalishnikov submachine gun.[2]

In 1994, Omar retired to the same small village of Singesar to devote his time and attention to the study of the Koran. One night the prophet Muhammad purportedly appeared to him in a dream and ordered him to put an end to the reign of terror of the warlords in Afghanistan.[3] The Afghan warlords were not only raping and pillaging the countryside, but were also blocking trade by setting up tollbooths along every road leading into a marketplace. Charging exorbitant tolls was an accepted practice in Afghanistan, and even the fee of two million afghanis (about US$300) for every truck from southern Pakistan to pass into Kabul could be overlooked. But other things were happening at the checkpoints that could not be ignored. Several toll collectors at the gates were dragging young men and boys (many of whom were Muslims) from trucks and cars, forcing them to undergo mock public marriages before sodomizing them repeatedly and collecting the fee to let them pass.[4]

Omar summoned fifty Pashtun students from the nearby *madrassahs* (religious schools) and set out, like an earnest Wyatt

Earp with a posse from Dodge City, to rectify matters. By a series of quick and daring raids, the Taliban gained control of the provinces of Uruzgan and Zabol.

As word of the conquests spread, more and more students from the *madrassahs* in Pakistan's Baluchistan Province crossed the border to join the movement. Over time, the motley band of fifty students became transformed into a full-fledged army of thirty thousand. To add momentum to the movement, the ISI, Pakistan's secret service, began providing massive assistance to the Taliban, including Kalishnikov assault rifles, ammunition, training, logistics, and combat support.

In January 1995, the Taliban took over Afghanistan's major poppy growing center, Helmand, without a shot being fired. In this way, they managed to cut off the flow of drug revenue to Gulbuddin Hekmatyar, Afghan's leading warlord and founder of the Hezb-e-Islami group. On February 14, Hekmatyar fled from his headquarters in Charasyab, south of Kabul, leaving behind his arsenal of sophisticated weapons, including stockpiles of rocket-propelled grenades (RPGs), machine guns, and Stinger surface-to-air missiles. The Taliban now stood in control of much of Afghanistan, including the sole non-Iranian route between the Indian Ocean and central Asia—a route that was to become the financial lifeline of al Qaeda.

On April 4, 1996, Mullah Omar appeared on a rooftop in Kabul, the capital city of Afghanistan, and wrapped himself in the cloak of the prophet Muhammad, one of Islam's most sacred relics in Islam, while the all-male crowd yelled, "Amir-ul Momineen" ("Commander of the Faithful"), the traditional title of a *caliph*. By accepting this title, Omar became the highest authority of the Sunni Muslims this side of paradise.[5] (The Sunnis make up approximately 85 percent of Islam, with the Shiites accounting for much of the rest. The split between these two factions occurred after the death of the prophet Muhammad. The Sunnis follow the practices of the first four caliphs or "successors" of the Arab world. The Shiites reject the legitimacy of these caliphs and follow the practices of Ali, Muhammad's son-in-law.)[6]

Five months of bloody battle later, the Taliban gained control of Kabul, driving from power Afghan president Burhanuddin Rabbani and his military commander, Ahmad Shah Massoud. As soon as victory was achieved, Mullah Omar ordered his soldiers to hunt down Mohammad Najibullah, the Afghan communist who had ruled the country from 1986 to 1992. Najibullah took refuge in a UN compound, but the Taliban paid no heed to diplomatic courtesies. They dragged Najibullah from the compound, beat and castrated him before dragging him through the streets of Kabul behind a jeep and placing him before a firing squad. Najibullah's body was left dangling for weeks from a traffic post, along with the body of his executed brother.[7]

General Massoud and his soldiers retreated to the Pashir Valley, where they regrouped to form the Northern Alliance, the only pocket of resistance to Omar's complete control of the country.[8] Massoud's position was strengthened when he gained the support of ousted warlord Hekmatyar, who became his prime minister. The struggle between the Taliban and the Northern Alliance was to rage unabated even after the assassination of Massoud by two Arabs posing as TV journalists on September 9, 2001, through the launching of Operation Enduring Freedom (America's code name for the "war on terror") on October 7, 2001, and beyond.

Under rule of the Taliban, Afghanistan was renamed the Islamic Emirate of Afghanistan, and *shariah* (Islamic law) in its strictest form was imposed on the people. Since all forms of Western technology were now outlawed, bearded students from the *madrassahs* raised massive bonfires of videocassettes, VCRs, and television sets in the marketplaces of towns and villages. Records, cassettes, and compact discs of American music were confiscated and crushed underfoot. Every form of pleasure—even the flying of kites—became prohibited. Women—dressed in full burqas with mesh covering their eyes—were reduced to the roles of breeders and slaves. Men, required to grow full-length beards, were forced at gunpoint to appear at the mosque for prayer five times a day.[9] Sexual intercourse outside wedlock was punishable by one hundred lashes or stoning to death; those who engaged in homosexual acts were crushed by the toppling of brick walls upon their naked bodies. The hands and feet of thieves were amputated in a stadium at Kabul every Friday at 3:30 PM to the cheers of thousands of onlookers.[10] By such means, after twenty years of chaos, law and order, as interpreted by Islamic law, finally came to the land.

Nonetheless, a double standard came to prevail within the new system of government. While the religious militia, with leather whips in hand, tirelessly patrolled the streets and bazaars in pursuit of violators of Islamic law, the stalls of opium dealers remained open on every street corner. While executioners beheaded apostates, infidels, rapists, and murderers in the stadiums, Afghan drug lords were permitted to sell their wares and become rich. The drug lords drove their all-terrain vehicles, imported at great expense, through the miserable streets of Kandahar and Kabul that had become open cesspools, replete with rancid garbage and raw sewage.[11]

From 1996 to 2001, Mullah Omar and the Taliban remained focused on one objective: the suppression of the Northern Alliance and the unification of Afghanistan under the white flag of Islamic purity. But this task proved to be impossible since Massoud had demonstrated that he was a master strategist. Every year when winter receded, the Taliban would set out across the Shomali plains to do battle with Massoud's forces but never achieved a decisive victory.

Enter bin Laden in May 1996, a few months before the Taliban takeover of Kabul. He had been deported from Sudan at the insistence of the United States and arrived in Jalalabad on board a Hercules C-130 cargo plane that had been specially outfitted for him, his wives, his children, and 150 al Qaeda associates.[12] Bin Laden wasted no time in establishing an alliance with Mullah Omar and the Taliban in Kabul. The alliance was forged for a variety of reasons. First, bin Laden was a great hero of the Afghan holy war. He had engaged in bloody hand-to-hand combat with Soviet soldiers at Jaji, near the Pakistani border, in 1986, and at Shaban in 1987. In 1989, bin Laden took part in the Jalalabad airport battle, where he was hit by shrapnel and earned his stripes as a *mujahed* ("holy war warrior"). He had earned these stripes under fire, not in a salon or a conference center.[13] What's more, he freely gave of his funds to recruit thousands of fighters, organize their transport, establish training camps, build fortifications along the Pakistani border, and dig tunnels that stretched for hundreds of miles throughout Afghanistan so that the fighters could get close to Northern Alliance soldiers without showing themselves.[14]

A second reason for the alliance was the fact that bin Laden was a Sunni brother who was seeking refuge under the Pashtun code of *milmastia*, or hospitality—a code that demanded the Taliban to protect bin Laden and his associates even at the risk of their own lives.[15]

Finally, bin Laden could provide the funds necessary for the defeat of the Northern Alliance and the conquest of Afghanistan. These funds would come from selling drugs through the ties that al Qaeda had made with Turkish officials and the Sicilian Mafia, not from bin Laden's personal fortune.[16]

In 1996, US security sources reported that bin Laden's net worth was in excess of $250 million.[17] This report was yet another example of governmental disinformation intended to portray bin

Laden as a solitary figure, a millionaire *mujahed* intent upon waging war against the Judeo-Christian world with his own financial resources. The truth was quite to the contrary. In 1995, when bin Laden was living in Sudan, he was experiencing severe financial problems, problems that could have spelled the end of his terrorist organization. Proof of this comes from the testimony at the 2001 trial in Manhattan of the al Qaeda operatives who were responsible for the bombing of the US embassies in Tanzania and Kenya. L'Houssaine Kherchtou, a key operative, mentioned that bin Laden admitted in 1994 that his financial resources were drained and that he had "lost all his money." At this time, Kherchtou said that the salaries and expenses of all group members were cut to the bone.[18] In 1996, bin Laden's personal pilot could not obtain funds to renew his pilot's license because money was "too tight."[19]

Bin Laden's financial woes were rooted in the fact that in 1994 the Saudi government revoked his citizenship and froze his assets. To make matters worse, bin Laden sunk vast sums of money into Sudan, including headquarters for family members and associates, training cells, road construction, agricultural projects, and an Islamic bank—assets that he was forced to relinquish when he was exiled in 1996.[20]

In Sudan, bin Laden also spent a considerable sum of money in his quest for weapons of mass destruction. On February 7, 2001, Jamal Ahmed al-Fadl, a Sudanese national and star witness for the prosecution in the trial of *The United States v. Osama bin Laden et alia*, told the court of his association with bin Laden and his terrorist group from 1992 to 1996. According to al-Fadl, he was singled out in 1994 to negotiate a deal for the purchase of uranium from two agents of the black market in Khartoum. One agent purportedly was Salah Abdel al-Mobruk, a lieutenant colonel in the Sudanese army and former government minister, and the other was a merchant named Basheer. The meeting was held in an office building on Jambouria Street. Al-Fadl said that he was told that the asking price for the uranium was $1.5 million, plus unspecified commissions for al-Mobruk and Basheer. The two agents said that the money had to be paid outside of Sudan. Al-Fadl relayed the terms to a top al Qaeda official, who, he said, found the terms acceptable as long as the uranium was tested to be weapons grade. A second meeting was held between al-Fadl and the two agents in a small house in the town of Bait al-Mal, north of Khartoum. Here, according to al-Fadl, he was shown a small cylinder between two and three feet tall with specification engravings indicating that it was of South African origin. After making arrangements for a test that was to be conducted with machinery and technicians from Nairobi, al-Fadl was informed by al Qaeda officials that the emir no longer would require his services. He was then paid $10,000, a sum that he considered paltry. The test of the uranium eventually was to be conducted in the town of Hilat Koko in Sudan, but al-Fadl was neither informed of the results nor the final outcome of the negotiations.[21]

The lure of Afghanistan for the financially strapped bin Laden resided not in the call from the minarets but rather the scent of the poppy fields. As his financial condition deteriorated, he turned to the *bubas*, the Turkish drug dealers, and the Sicilian Mafia with a proposal for the production of choice Number Four heroin in laboratories that he intended to establish outside Kabul.

Prior to bin Laden's return, the Golden Crescent of Iran, Pakistan, and Afghanistan, under the control of warlord Hekmatyar, could produce only low-grade Number Three heroin that was good only for smoking and snorting. This production process began when the petals from the poppies fell, exposing egg-shaped seed pods. The pods were sliced vertically to extract the opaque, milky sap—opium in its crudest form. As it darkened and became thicker, the extracted sap was pressed into bricks of opium gum. At Hekmatyar's refineries, the opium gum became mixed with lime in vats of boiling water. A precipitate of organic waste sank to the bottom, while the white morphine rose to the top. The morphine was drawn from the vats, reheated with ammonia, filtered, and boiled again until it became reduced to a brown paste. The paste was poured into mounds and dried in the sun. The finished product was now ready for delivery to the Turkish merchants. The entire process could be performed with primitive technology and a modicum of expertise.

But the international drug market now called for Number Four that could be mainlined into the veins. This refinement required the talents of highly skilled chemists working in sophisticated facilities. The opium paste had to be heated and processed with acetic anhydride for six hours in glass containers to form diacetylmorphine. Water and chloroform were then added to precipitate impurities. The solution was drained and sodium carbonate added to make the heroin solidify and sink. The heroin was then filtered from the sodium carbonate solution through activated charcoal and purified with alcohol. The product was then heated to evaporate the alcohol and leave the heroin. Next came the tricky stage—mixing the heroin with ether and hydrochloric acid, a process that would produce a violent explosion if handled by an improperly trained technician. The final product—Number Four heroin—was a fluffy white powder that would be shipped in twenty- to one-hundred-kilo packages.

According to the terms of the agreement, bin Laden would take over the poppy fields that Hekmatyar had been forced to abandon. He would establish sophisticated laboratories near Kabul and reopen the trade route to the West. The *bubas* and the Sicilian Mafia, knowing that Number Four heroin was worth one hundred times more than Number Three, were more than happy to invest in the proposed venture. For this reason, bin Laden's first recruits, upon landing in Kabul with his entourage, were not soldiers from the *mujahadeen* but chemists from the former Soviet Union, who had joined the growing horde of unemployed workers. At the same time, bin Laden approached, through intermediaries, major landowners in the opium growing districts of Afghanistan with offers to buy "all the opium they could grow."[22]

Within months the facilities were up and running as the civil war continued to rage throughout the country. The laboratories soon became capable of producing five thousand metric tons of heroin a year, making bin Laden the world's largest supplier of the new international drug of choice. By 1997, the poppy harvest in Afghanistan soared to 3,276 tons of raw opium, and revenues began to pour into the coffers of al Qaeda at a rate estimated between $5 billion and $16 billion a year.[23] By 1998, the National Household Survey discovered 149,000 new heroin users throughout the United States who required treatment for their addiction. Eighty percent of the new addicts were under the age of twenty-six. The average new addict was spending from $150 to $200 a day to maintain his habit.[24] While the drug trade increased to new highs in the United States, it began to boom beyond belief in Europe. From 1996 to 2001, the Europeans consumed more than fifteen tons of heroin a year—twice the amount that was sold in America. The source of the new supply was no secret. "Terrorism, organized crime, and the illegal trade are one interrelated problem," Abdurakhim Kakharov, a deputy interior minister of Tajikistan, told a congressional committee in Washington on September 6, 2001. "The terrorist groups and the drugs are exported from the same source—Afghanistan."[25]

The heroin was transported by truck caravans from Afghanistan, through northern Iran (thanks to bin Laden's contacts with Hezbollah, the Shiite terrorist group) and Turkey, to Sofia, the capital city of Bulgaria, where the wheelers and dealers of the international drug trade—the *bubas* and the *mafiosi*—resided in comfortable villas or government guest houses. "The drug dealers reside openly in Sofia, maintaining flamboyant and free-spending lifestyles," John Lawn, the former director of the Drug Enforcement Administration, told a congressional committee in 1998. "Their presence is so obvious and their deals so flagrant that it is impossible not to conclude they are enjoying official protection."[26]

In Sophia, on any given day, one could find agents of such purported Sicilian dons as Luciano Liggio, Salvatore Riina, and Bernardo Provenzano of Corleone and Nitto Santapaola and the Ferrar brothers from Catania in the opulent lobby of the Hotel Vitosha, negotiating deals with Turkish merchants over the latest shipments from Afghanistan.[27]

Bin Laden made connections with the Chechen brothers Shamil and Shirvani Basayev to reestablish the so-called Abkhaz drug route.[28] This circuitous route led from Afghanistan through Khorog in Tajikistan and Osh in Kyrgyzstan along a treacherous mountain road to the Vedensky Rayon in Chechnya. From this central location, Abkhaz trucks and Mi-6 helicopters transported the product to the port city of Sukhumi in the breakaway Georgian province of Abkhazia, where it was loaded on Turkish ships and shipped to the port of Famagusta in northern Cyprus. Here it was broken down into small packets for distribution to Europe and the United States.[29]

The drug connection appeared to be the realization of an utmost irony—an incredible fantasy beyond the imaginative power of any modern Scheherazade. The United States, in the eyes of al Qaeda, would become a victim of its own decadence. Every small bag of smack sold in America would serve to transform an obscure engineer from Saudi Arabia, albeit from a prominent and wealthy construction family, into the greatest warrior to arise from Islam since the time of Saladin. "The drug trade is a triple-pronged weapon for bin Laden and the Taliban," Rachel Ehrenfeld, director of the Center for the Study of Corruption, told the press. "It finances their activities. It undermines the enemy. And it proves that the enemy is corrupt, which they then use in their own recruiting propaganda."[30]

Thanks to Western decadence, bin Laden began to earn an amount estimated anywhere from $500 million to $1 billion a year.[31] He could now purchase through his Russian connections the objects of his heart's desire: several nuclear suitcases and the requisite nuclear technology that would bring about the triumphant "Day of Islam," when all of creation would fall in submission before the judgment seat of Allah.

CHAPTER 2

THE NUCLEAR SUITCASES

Remember your Lord inspired the angels with the message:

I am with you: give firmness to the Believers: I will inspire terror in the hearts of Unbelievers: you smite them above their necks and smite all their fingertips off them.

—Koran 8:2

In compliance with God's order, we issue the following fatwa to all Muslims: The ruling to kill Americans and their allies—civilians and military—is an individual duty for every Muslim who can do it in any country in which it is possible to do it, in order to liberate the Al-Aqsa Mosque and the holy mosque in Mecca from their grip, and in order for their armies to move out of all the lands of Islam, defeated and unable to threaten any Muslim. This is in accordance with the words of Almighty Allah, "and fight the pagans all together as they fight you all together" and "fight them until there is no more tumult or oppression, and there prevail justice and faith in Allah."

—World Islamic Statement,
Jihad against Jews and Crusaders
February 23, 1998

The information about the nuclear suitcases that are meant to destroy the United States of America came from Boris M and Alexy D, two members of the Chechen Mafia from Little Odessa. The Russian émigrés appeared unrestrained, almost feral, in their behavior. They chain-smoked Marlboros in nonsmoking areas of restaurants, consumed vodka like soda pop as they drove their stolen Mercedes S-Class from place to place, and spouted sexual obscenities—replete with gestures implying fellatio, cunnilingus, or masturbation—to various women they encountered on the street and in shopping malls and office buildings. Short and quick, they moved like ferrets. With their rounded shoulders and skinny arms covered with homemade tattoos, their physical presence was unimpressive, almost comic, until you noticed their scarred faces, their broken teeth, and their incredibly pale eyes like those of wild animals—wolves from the steppes—piercing and unblinking eyes that displayed no spark of civility or compassion.

Boris and Alexy never seemed to wash their hair, clean their nails, change their clothes, or trim their facial hair, including the nicotine-stained mustaches that covered their thin lips. To complement their unkempt appearance, they emitted mechanical laughter at regular intervals as though they were doing imitations of Richard Widmark in *Kiss of Death* for their own amusement.

The two Russians came to northeastern Pennsylvania to settle a business matter for their boss in Coney Island. Wiseguys from Pittston, purported members of the Bufalino crime family, had tried to act tough with some well-heeled Russian businessmen over a real estate deal concerning timeshares in New York City. Believing they had been cheated out of $750,000, the Pittston thugs traveled to the Big Apple, made a lot of threats, and slapped a few faces. The wiseguys thought they had straightened the matter out and returned

to Pittston to await the arrival of a courier with the cash. But neither the courier nor the check arrived.

Instead, Boris and Alexy reportedly showed up at the headquarters of a capo of the Bufalino clan, with Colt Anacondas stuffed in
their pants. The capo had stiff knees and he never buckled under
pressure—not even when the feds placed him in a hot seat over
some hits in Philadelphia. But the two Russians, with their ice-cold
eyes and Richard Widmark routines, gave him a case of the jitters.
He dropped his tough guy act and became nice and polite.

After the capo graciously forgave the debt, Boris and Alexy
became regular visitors to northeastern Pennsylvania as part of a
stolen car ring. Members of the ring combed the inventory of junkyards throughout the country for late-model foreign and domestic
cars—Cadillac Escalades and Eldorados, Lincoln Navigators and
Town Cars, BMW Roadsters, Chevy Corvettes, Jaguars, Ferraris, and
Porsche Boxsters. They preferred vehicles that insurance companies
wrote off as total wrecks—vehicles that could be purchased for a
thousand or two in cash. They hauled the wrecks, which were the
same models as their stolen cars, to garages and chop shops in Pennsylvania and New Jersey. They switched serial numbers, repainted the
stolen cars, washed titles by transferring ownership across state lines,
and sold the choice cars to a clientele of yuppies who wanted to
project an image of wealth and success for a bargain-basement price.
It was a neat and highly lucrative scheme. Since some of the largest
junkyards in the country are located among the abandoned coal mines
of Scranton, Boris and Alexy discovered northeastern Pennsylvania
to be highly advantageous for their unique line of work.[1]

The two Russians, along with other members of the Mafia from
Little Odessa, were also involved in drug trafficking. They dealt
almost exclusively in heroin that flowed into the United States from
the harbor city of Gdansk, Poland. The drugs came to Poland from
opium merchants in Turkey, who obtained the product from the

Helmand and Nangarhar provinces of Afghanistan. There farmers cultivated the poppy fields and harvested the crops, which they sold to the drug lords, who operated the laboratories where the flowers were cut to extract the gum, and where the gum was refined into high-quality Number Four heroin—the preferred drug of choice for the American and European markets. Boris and Alexy didn't know or care where the drugs came from. They only knew that the Scranton/Wilkes-Barre airport in Avoca, a place that hosts only one major airline, had international arrival/departure status and few customs officials, making it a prime place for drugs to enter the country. For many years, Rik Luytjes, one of America's most successful drug dealers, purportedly operated a flight of cargo planes called Air America to import millions of tons of cocaine into Avoca without any airport official ever batting an eye, let alone opening any of the crate of "choice Colombian" that bore the image of Juan Valdes and his mule.[2]

Along with the drugs and stolen cars, the two Russians sold a wide array of weapons at rock-bottom prices. For three hundred dollars, Boris and Alexy could provide a customer with an unregistered Saturday night special—a .38 Harrington or Richardson; and, for less than five thousand dollars, an Uzi or AK-47. For more demanding customers, they offered Stalin Organ–style rocket launchers for ten thousand dollars, less if bought in volume. Other items at bargain prices included land mines, antiaircraft guns, bazookas, and, for fifty bucks, fountain pen guns that could be used to fire a single bullet or to write a ransom note.

It was guns—not cars or drugs—that enabled the Russian Mafia to prosper into a multibillion-dollar enterprise. Boris and Alexy worked for a former Soviet official named David Z, the *pakhan*, or boss, of the Chechen clan in Coney Island.

One sale, according to Boris and Alexy, made David Z a very wealthy man, so wealthy that he moved his entire operation to New

York; so wealthy that he obtained green cards for his criminal associates by arranging marriages to plump and pink-cheeked women from Coney Island who had obtained their American citizenship and were willing to wed and bed—sight unseen—any émigré from Mother Russia for the right price.

In 1996, David Z and his Mafia associates in Chechnya allegedly purchased a shipment of Special Atomic Demolition Munitions (SADMs), or "nuclear suitcases," from former KGB officials who preferred *perestreika* (the Russian word for "shootout") to *perestroika* (Mikhail Gorbachev's word for "reform"). The compact nukes represented the most desirable weapons for customers from such countries as Iran, North Korea, and Libya, and representatives of the World Islamic Front who wanted a big bang for their buck. The Chechen Mafia purportedly sold twenty nuclear suitcases in Grozny to representatives of Osama bin Laden and the *mujahadeen*. For the weapons, bin Laden paid $30 million in cash and two tons of heroin that had been refined in his laboratories in Afghanistan. The street value of the heroin was in excess of $700 million.

News of the sale was not only conveyed to US officials by Russia's Federal Security Service but also leaked to the press. The story appeared on August 16, 1998, in the *London Times*,[3] and, several weeks later, in such publications as the *Jerusalem Report, Al-Watan Al-Arabi, Muslim Magazine*, and *Al-Majallah* (London's Saudi weekly).[4]

In 2002, *Al-Majallah* published an update, claiming that bin Laden had succeeded in obtaining a total of forty-eight nuclear suitcases from the Russian Mafia over the course of several years.[5] This claim was supported by reports from Israeli intelligence that al Qaeda agents purchased twelve to fifteen kilos of uranium-235 six months before September 11 from Semion Mogilevich, a shadowy Ukrainian-born Jew who rules over a vast crime empire of arms trafficking, money laundering, drug running, and white slavery. For the additional nukes, Mogilevich reportedly collected more than $75 million from bin Laden and his associates.[6]

The nuclear suitcases were originally designed to serve as tactical rather than strategic weapons for use against NATO targets in time of war. They were not really suitcases, but suitcase-sized nuclear devices, which could be fired from grenade or rocket launchers or detonated in public buildings, shopping malls, arenas, or stadiums for sporting events. One weapon placed in the center of a major metropolitan area was capable of instantly killing several hundred thousand civilians while exposing millions of others to lethal gamma rays.[7]

Some of these weapons were smuggled into the United States by Soviet agents and buried at scattered, remote locations. "There is no doubt that the Soviets stored material [including nuclear suitcases] in this country," Curt Weldon (R-PA), chairman of the House Armed Services Subcommittee on Military Research and Development, said. "The question is what and where."[8]

In attempting to verify the reports of the buried nukes, FBI director Louis Freeh ordered a team of nuclear technicians to excavate several areas around Brainerd, Minnesota, where Soviet spies were believed to have forward-deployed several suitcases in case of war.[9]

Diggings began at additional sites after KGB defector Vasili Mitrokhin, who served as a chief archivist for the agency, informed British intelligence that secret stockpiles of tactical nuclear devices were buried in upstate New York, California, Texas, and Minnesota.[10]

Mitrakhin's information was supported by Col. Stanislav Lunev, the highest-ranking military spy to defect from the Soviet Union and the leading confidential source on Russia's nuclear arsenal. Lunev told a congressional committee in January 2000 that nuclear suitcases had indeed been buried in the United States, although he could not pinpoint the exact locations. Such information remains secret, Lunev said, because Russian military leaders continue to believe that a nuclear conflict between Russia and the United States remains "inevitable." He concluded his testimony by saying: "And just now what we are talking about, location of technical nuclear devices, these places we have selected extremely carefully for a long, long period of time, and to believe it is possible to find these places just like that without using extremely, extremely large resources of the country, I don't think that it would be realistic until the Russian government, which still has the keys to these locations, will disclose their locations."[11]

The number of weapons buried in the United States and Europe remains anyone's guess. But Soviet scientists produced more than seven hundred nuclear suitcases during the 1960s and 1970s and hundreds more during the 1980s. The first SADMs were very expensive to maintain and too heavy for practical use. They had to be carried in crates that measured 4 feet by 2.5 feet with a weight that exceeded eight hundred pounds. During the 1970s, the weapons were streamlined so that they could be transported in cases measuring 2 feet by 1.5 feet with a weight of 320 pounds. These modified nukes consisted of three coffee-can-sized aluminum canisters that had to be connected by a crew of five—a commander, a radio officer, and three army technicians—before detonation.[12] The bombs were carried in green canvas cases with pockets on the side. The detonator was about six inches long and was carried in a "knifelike" sheath."[13] Each weapon could produce an explosive yield of at least one kiloton—enough to topple not only the Twin Towers but also much of lower Manhattan.

Throughout the Cold War, the United States developed similar small nukes that became known as "rucksack bombs" or "Davy Crocketts." In 1966 the Department of Defense made a training film that showed how the SADMs could be stuffed into the parachutes of commandos and attached to the diving gear of Navy SEALs. The film also demonstrated how the small weapons could be affixed to buildings, bridges, and ships and detonated by a team of highly trained military personnel.[14]

During the 1980s, Soviet and US nuclear technicians respectively made refinements until the weapons came to measure 24 inches by 16 inches by 8 inches with a weight of less than sixty pounds. A single agent could now transport the device from place to place in a suitcase to cause a significant "event." Each small "suitcase" contained at least one kiloton of fissionable plutonium and uranium. The plutonium and uranium were kept in separate compartments and connected to a triggering mechanism that could be activated by a clock or a call from a cell phone.[15]

The small Soviet nukes, however, lacked the safety systems to prevent unauthorized use. To rectify this problem, the weapons were equipped with electronic combination locks that could be opened and operated only by SPETSNAZ (Soviet special forces) personnel. As added security, they were placed under the care of the Ninth Directorate of the KGB, a unit responsible for executive protection, rather than the Ministry of Defense. For this reason, the weapons never appeared on the list of the Soviet nuclear arsenal.[16] Few in the United States, including the ambassadors engaged in disarmament talks with Russian officials, knew of their existence.

After the collapse of the Soviet Union in 1991, Russian army units, tired of polishing their ICBMs and rotating their nuclear weapons, decided to manifest the new spirit of capitalism by stripping the weapons down into economically attractive parcels and selling them to the highest bidders. By 1993, over 6,430 reports of stolen weapons, ranging from assault rifles to tanks, were filed by the Russian Defense Ministry. By 1998, the ministry received more than seven hundred reports of nuclear material being sold to various buyers within and outside of Mother Russia.[17]

Many Russian army officers were becoming incredibly rich. On the black market, a kilo of chromium-50 sold for $25,000; cesium-137 for $1 million; and lithium-6 for $10 million, all of which are needed to build nuclear weapons.[18]

Former members of the KGB, which had been replaced by the FSB, also took part in the sale of goodies from the Soviet arsenal. These agents could provide buyers with some of the most highly prized items, including the nuclear suitcases that had been placed in their care. Such sophisticated weaponry would be of little use to rogue nations or terrorist groups without technical expertise. But as Russia transformed itself from a superpower to a third world nation in less than six years, such technology was becoming readily available. By 1996, more than three thousand unpaid and disillusioned Russian scientists with expertise in the construction and maintenance of weapons of mass destruction left the country. Some went to North Korea, Libya, and Iran. Others obtained lucrative employment with al Qaeda and other Muslim terrorist groups. By 1996, the likelihood of a nuclear device exploding in America increased to a red alert level—the highest since the Cuban missile crisis.[19]

Concern about the nuclear suitcases first arose in 1994, when Dzhokhar Dudayev, leader of the Chechen separatists, notified the US State Department that he possessed tactical nuclear suitcases. Dudayev said that he was willing to sell to hostile countries or groups if the United States failed to recognize Chechnya's independence. His claim was granted credence by officials from the National Intelligence Council, an umbrella organization for the US analytical community. The officials told a congressional committee that there were at least four occasions between 1992 and 1996 when weapons-grade and weapons-usable nuclear materials, including SADMs, had been stolen from Soviet stockpiles. "Of these thefts," the officials said, "we assess that undetected smuggling has occurred, although we do not know the extent or the magnitudes."[20]

Dudayev's demands were not met, and in 1996 the Chechen Mafia negotiated the sale of the suitcases to representatives of Osama bin Laden. It was an amicable deal between Muslims. Bin Laden got the weapons to destroy the Great Satan (the United States) and the Chechens got the cash to drive away the Russian Bear.

In addition to his cadre of Russian scientists, bin Laden recruited former SPETSNAZ troops to work on the project of preparing the delivery of the suitcases to major cities in Europe and the United States. To simplify the process of activation, the technicians and scientists came up with a way of hot-wiring the bombs to the bodies of Muslim soldiers who long for immediate martyrdom and elevation to seventh heaven.[21]

In 1998, Alexander Lebed, the former Russian security secretary under Boris Yeltsin, met in a closed-door session with members of the US House of Representatives and admitted that forty nuclear suitcases had disappeared from the Russian arsenal and could be in the hands of Muslim extremists. Lebed said that he was able to confirm the production of 132 suitcases and could account for only 48. When asked the whereabouts of the other 84 suitcases, Lebed replied: "I have no idea." He went on to testify that he did not know how many suitcases had been produced throughout the Cold War, but said that the later models of the small atomic demolition munitions were "ideal weapons for nuclear terror."[22]

Lebed's testimony was later corroborated by Vladimir Denisov, a former member of the Russian Security Council, and by Aleksey Yablokov, Environment Adviser to Russian president Boris Yeltsin. Denisov told a US congressional committee that he had received numerous reports that the missing nukes had been obtained by the Chechen separatists.[23] Yablokov testified that over seven hundred suitcases had been produced exclusively for the KGB. For this reason, he explained, the nuclear suitcases did not appear on the official inventory of Russia's nuclear weapons. He added that the small nukes would have required two major overhauls in the twenty or so years since they had been manufactured and did not know if such overhauls had been conducted.[24]

In the wake of these revelations, Yeltsin signed a set of amendments to the Russian Federation Law on State Secrets that classified all information about military nuclear weapons and facilities to contain fears about the missing nukes.[25]

The weapons that Lebed described, according to physicist Carey Sublette of the Nuclear Weapon Archive, are based on a nuclear design concept called linear implosion. This concept is that an elongated (football-shaped), lower-density subcritical mass of material can be compressed and deformed into a critical, higher-density spherical configuration by embedding it in a cylinder of explosives that are initiated at each end. As the detonation progresses from each end toward the middle, the fissile mass is squeezed into a supercritical shape. Any 155 mm artillery shell, if shortened by omitting the nonessential conical ogive and fuse, would fit diagonally in Lebed's suitcase.[26] The device would be capable of producing an explosive yield of ten kilotons—enough to wipe away much of New York City—if the fusion was boosted by a thin beryllium reflector with a thickness no greater than the core radius. Sublette believes that the weapons could be further refined to fit into an attaché case.[27]

In 1998, Yossef Bodansky, head of the Congressional Task Force on Terrorism and Unconventional Warfare in Washington, DC, told a congressional committee: "There is no longer much doubt that bin Laden has succeeded in his quest for nuclear suicide bombs." He told the committee that the bombs had been transported through Pakistan to various al Qaeda cells. "The Russians believe he [bin Laden] has a handful [of nuclear weapons], the

Saudi intelligence services are very conservative, perhaps they are friendly to the United States, believe that he has in the neighborhood of twenty. As far as the acquisition and obtaining [of such weapons], there's the multiple sources of that, dealing with the actual purchase of the suitcase bombs. He [bin Laden] has a collection of individuals knowledgeable in activating the bombs and he is looking for and recruiting former Soviet Special Forces in learning how to operate the bombs behind enemy lines."

Asked about the immediacy of the threat, Bodansky said: "We don't have any indication that they are going to use it [the nuclear arsenal] tomorrow or any other day. But they have the capacity; they have the legitimate authorization; they have the logic for using it. So, one does not go into the tremendous amount of expenditures, effort, investment in human beings and in human resources, to have something that will be kept in storage for a rainy day."[28]

Word also came straight from the horse's mouth. To inform the world of his possession of the weapons, bin Laden issued a statement called "The Nuclear Bombs of Islam" in which he said: "It is the duty of Muslims to prepare as much force as possible to terrorize the enemies of God."[29] In a December 1999 interview with journalists from *Time* magazine, he let it be known in an oblique way that he had secured nuclear weapons. "Acquiring weapons for the defense of Muslims is a religious duty," he said. "If I have indeed acquired these weapons, then I thank God for enabling me to do so."[30]

Several weeks later, when asked by ABC News if he was seeking to obtain chemical and nuclear weapons, bin Laden said: "If I seek to acquire such weapons, this is a religious duty. How we use them is up to us."[31]

In an interview with Hamid Mir in November 2001, bin Laden was even more explicit. "We have chemical and nuclear weapons," he told the Pakistani editor. "If America uses chemical or nuclear weapons against us, then we may retort with chemical or nuclear weapons." When Mir asked the Muslim imam where he obtained such weapons, bin Laden said: "Go on to the next question." Bin Laden told Mir that it was relatively easy for al Qaeda to obtain nuclear weapons. "It is not difficult, not if you have contacts in Russia and with other militant groups. They are available for $10 million and $20 million." At this stage in the interview, Ayman al-Zawahiri, bin Laden's chief strategist, interjected: "If you go to BBC reports, you will find that thirty nuclear weapons are missing from Russia's nuclear arsenal." Al-Zawahiri added: "We have links with Russia's underworld channels."[32]

But Boris and Alexy, who are Muslims (albeit not fundamentalists) and who speak *Nakh* (the language of Chechens), remain unconcerned about the plans and schemes of bin Laden and the *mujahadeen*, as they continue to enjoy the "good life" in America, while going about their business of selling stolen cars and choice heroin from Afghanistan. They are well aware of the transaction that might cause the next 9/11.

"We love the USA," Boris says. He is behind the wheel of a stolen BMW with several plastic bags of choice heroin in the glove compartment and a shipment of Uzis, AK-47s, and other weapons (including land mines) in the trunk. It is Labor Day weekend. The traffic on Route 80 between New York City and Scranton, Pennsylvania, is heavy. In the backseat, Alexy takes a slug of Stoli and chants, "USA, USA." Boris takes a drag of his Marlboro, flashes his yellow teeth, and breaks into his best Richard Widmark imitation. Alexy joins in. They continue to emit the forced laughter for several minutes until their voices seem to meld into a howl.

CHAPTER 3

FATWAS, FUMBLES, AND FAILURES

*Every grown-up Muslim hates Americans, Jews, and Christians.
It is part of our belief and our religion. Since I was a boy, I have
been at war with and harboring hatred of Americans.*
                                        —Osama bin Laden, 1998

*America has made many accusations against us. Its charge that
we are carrying out acts of terrorism is unwarranted. If inciting
people to do that is terrorism and if killing those who kill our sons
is terrorism, then let history be witness that we are terrorists.*
                                        —Osama bin Laden, 2002

In addition to purchasing portable nuclear weapons from the Russian Mafia in Chechnya, bin Laden also used his newly recovered wealth to fund multimillion-dollar projects throughout Kandahar that would serve to strengthen public support for the Taliban. These projects included the installation of new water and sewage systems, the restoration and expansion of electrical service, the construction of a new commercial center, the building of a massive mosque on the site of an old movie theater (since movies were now prohibited), and the erection of a large housing project in the Saudi style with pink and green pinnacles. Bin Laden also supervised the renovation of a nineteenth-century palace as living quarters for Mullah Omar, his wives, and his children. In addition, he financed the expansion of the airport with new runways to support heavy aircraft.

To further solidify his ties to Mullah Omar, bin Laden developed a guerilla unit of two thousand Arabs, known as the 055 Brigade, to assist the Taliban in their fight against the Northern Alliance.

Along with these undertakings, bin Laden established a permanent base of operations called Najim al-Jihad ("Star of the Holy War") near Jalalabad, and converted a complex of caves into an intricate hideout that remained guarded at all times by five hundred al Qaeda soldiers. The complex, stripped of all creaturely comforts, included a network of computers, a satellite telephone system, and a library of vintage Islamic works.

From his new refuge, bin Laden issued a host of radical pronouncements, beginning on August 23, 1996, with "The Declaration of War against the Americans Occupying the Land of the Two Holy Places." This rambling statement against the American military presence in Arabia featured an analysis of American policy in the Middle East since World War II. It condemned the Saudi regime for its corruption and its anti-Islamic policies. It also provided the opinions of Muslim scholars about the relationships between pious believers and infidels.

Bin Laden concluded his declaration of war with a call to arms: "My Muslim brothers of the world, your brothers in Palestine and the land of the two Holy Places are calling upon you to take part in fighting against the enemy, your enemy and their enemy, the Americans and the Israelis: they are asking you to do whatever you can, with one's own means and ability, to expel the enemy, humiliated and defeated, out of the sanctities of Islam." The fatwa was signed

Osama bin Muhammad bin Laden "from the peaks of the Hindu Kush, Afghanistan." It was written on an Apple Macintosh—the computer that bore the advertising motto "Think different."[1]

The fatwa contained the first expression of Osama's vision of an Islamic utopia—the establishment of a global *khalifa*, or "caliphate," with roots in Afghanistan. Not since the demise of the Ottoman Empire at the close of World War I had there been an attempt to create a union of the *ummas* ("true believers") throughout the Middle East and central Asia under the green flag of Islam.[2] The union would be established by war and the *khalifa* would rise like a phoenix from the ashes of the United States of America and Judeo-Christian civilization.

Khaled al-Fawwaz, bin Laden's director of communications, dispatched copies of the fatwa to the international press and made arrangements for selected journalists to visit bin Laden in Afghanistan.[3]

In March 1997, bin Laden gave his first television interview to journalists from CNN in a cave near Jalalabad. During the interview, he railed in Arabic against the injustices inflicted upon the Muslim people by the United States. "We declared *jihad* against the US government," he said, while sipping a cup of tea, "because the US government has committed acts that are extremely unjust, hideous, and criminal, whether directly or through its support of the Israeli occupation. And we believe the United States is directly responsible for those who were killed in Palestine, Lebanon, and Iraq. This US government abandoned humanitarian feelings by these hideous crimes. It transgressed all bounds and behaved in a way not witnessed before by any power or any imperialist power in the world."[4]

Between 1996 and 1998, bin Laden spent millions from his drug trade to form the International Islamic Front for *Jihad* against the Jews and Crusaders, a coalition of various terrorist groups, including Egypt's al-Jihad and al-Gama'a al-Islamiyya; Pakistan's

53

Jamiat ul-Ulema, Jaish Mohammed, Hezb ul-Mujahideen, Lashkar-e-Toiba, al-Hadith, Harakat ul-Ansar, and al-Badar; Afghanistan's Ulema Union; Somalia's al-Ittihad al-Islami; the Moro Islamic Liberation Front and Abu Sayyaf of the Philippines; Kashmir's Partisan Movement; the Libyan Islamic Group; Lebanon's Partisans League, Hezbollah, and Asbat al-Ansar; the al-Jihad Group of Yemen; the Islamic Movement of Uzbekistan; Jordan's Bayt al-Imam; the Islamic Jihad and Hamas of Palestine; Algeria's Saafi Group for Proselytism and Combat and the Armed Islamic Group; and the Groupe Roubaix of France and Canada.[5]

Bin Laden had created a hydra. During the course of the holy war against the United States and Israel, one terrorist group, upon attack, would transmogrify into another. When the head of al Qaeda was severed, the head of al-Jihad would appear; al-Jihad would give rise to Jamiat ul-Ulema, so that efforts to defeat any Islamic terrorist group would represent an exercise in futility. He established training camps for terrorists throughout eastern Afghanistan as well as terrorist cells in fifty-five countries throughout the world, including the United States and Canada, so that the hydra would not be confined to a single lair.[6] When destroyed in one locale, it would reappear in another.

In February 1998, on behalf of the International Islamic Front, bin Laden issued his second fatwa with the following declaration: "The ruling to kill the Americans and their allies—civilians and military—is an individual duty for every Muslim who can do it in any country in which it is possible to do it, in order to liberate the Al-Aqsa Mosque and the holy mosque in Mecca from their grip, and in order for their armies to move out of all of the lands of Islam, defeated and unable to threaten any Muslim. This is in accordance with the words of Almighty Allah, 'and fight the pagans all together as they fight you all together,' and 'fight them until there is no more tumult or oppression, and there prevail justic and faith in Allah.'"[7]

In the fatwa, bin Laden gave three reasons why Muslims throughout the world must unite in a holy war against the United States:

First, for seven years the United States has been occupying the lands of Islam in the holiest of places, the Arabian Peninsula, plundering its riches, dictating to its rulers, humiliating its people, terrorizing its neighbors, and turning its bases in the Peninsula into a spearhead through which to fight the neighboring Muslim peoples. If some people have formerly debated the fact of the occupation, all the people of the Peninsula have now acknowledged it. The best proof of this is the Americans' continuing aggression against the Iraqi people using the Peninsula as a staging post, even though all its rulers are against their territories being used to that end, still they are helpless.

Second, despite the great devastation inflicted on the Iraqi people by the Crusader-Zionist alliance, and despite the huge number of those killed, in excess of 1 million. . . despite all this, the Americans are once again trying to repeat the horrific massacres, as though they are not content with the protracted blockade imposed after the ferocious war or the fragmentation and devastation. So now they come to annihilate what is left of this people and to humiliate their Muslim neighbors.

Third, if the Americans' aims behind these wars are religious and economic, the aim is also to serve the Jews' petty state and divert attention from its occupation of Jerusalem and murder of Muslims there. The best proof of this is their eagerness to destroy Iraq, the strongest neighboring Arab state, and their endeavor to fragment all the states of the region such as Iraq, Saudi Arabia, Egypt, and Sudan into paper statelets and through their disunion and weakness to guarantee Israel's survival and the continuation of the brutal Crusade occupation of the Peninsula.[8]

On August 7, 1998, as proof of the earnestness of his intent, bin Laden ordered the bombings of the US embassies in Kenya and

Tanzania, killing 234 people, twelve of them American, and wounding over five thousand others. The plans of al Qaeda operatives to bomb a third US embassy—this one in Kampala, Uganda— was prevented by a tip from a CIA informant.[9]

Thirteen days later, on August 20, US forces retaliated by firing a host of cruise missiles at al Qaeda residential and military complexes. The United States also targeted the al-Shifa Pharmaceutical Plant near Khartoum, believing it to be a laboratory for the production of the deadly nerve agent VX.[10] From the Oval Office, President Clinton addressed the nation by saying: "Our mission was clear; to strike at the network of radical groups affiliated with and funded by Osama bin Laden, perhaps the preeminent organizer and financier of international terrorism in the world today. . . . Earlier today, the United States carried out simultaneous strikes against terrorist facilities and infrastructure in Afghanistan. It contained key elements of bin Laden's network and infrastructure and has served as the training camp for literally thousands of terrorists around the globe. We have reason to believe that a gathering of key terrorist leaders was to take place there today, thus underscoring the urgency of our actions. Our forces also attacked a factory in Sudan associated with the bin Laden network. The factory was involved in the production of materials for chemical weapons."[11]

But the key terrorist leaders were not gathering in Afghanistan. Bin Laden, al-Zawahiri, and other al Qaeda leaders were not in the camps at Khost. They were safe and secure in a Pakistani *madrassah*. Although the missiles did hit bin Laden's camps, the only casualties were locals and some low-level militants.[12] The camps themselves had been constructed of stone, wood, and mud, making it easy for bin Laden's soldiers to rebuild them in a matter of days. Nor was the Sudan factory involved in the production of materials for chemical weapons. The plant simply produced common pharmaceuticals, including ibuprofen.[13]

In response to the bombing by America, al-Gama'a al-Islamiyya in Egypt issued the following statement on behalf of the World Islamic Front:

> Your crime will not go unpunished! With missiles and planes, the Americans have carried out the largest terrorist operation in the world. Bombs were dropped yesterday on Sudan and Afghanistan killing women and children and destroying a pharmaceutical factory. These are the same bombs that were dropped on a shelter in Iraq [an American missile accidentally pierced through the Armariya shelter in Baghdad on February 13, 1991, incinerating more than twelve hundred men, women, and children].
>
> The White House is drowning in a sea of shame and crimes. The Americans are unable to confront the *mujahadeen* [warriors in a jihad] on a battlefield. Muslims must support Sudan and Afghanistan. We must surround American embassies in the Arab countries and force Arab leaders to close them, because they are nests of spies. The Americans must stop applauding their leaders when they kill Muslims.[14]

The US attack was more than a resounding dud —several of the bombs even failed to detonate upon impact. It proved to be a rallying call to Muslims throughout the Middle East for the holy war. The camps contained five mosques to provide religious services not only to the *mujahadeen* but also to local villagers. Four mosques were destroyed, leaving "the burned pages of two hundred Korans" throughout the area. Pictures of the bombed mosques and burned pages were distributed throughout the Muslim world. "America has invited death upon itself," Mauvi Fazlur Rehman Khalil, head of Harakat ul-Ansar, told the press. "If we don't get justice from the world court we know how to get our own justice."[15]

The Clinton administration's missile attack on Afghanistan served only to enhance bin Laden's image as a righteous warrior.

Rahimullah Yusufzai, the Pakistani journalist who interviewed bin Laden for ABC News, noted: "In an Islamic world desperately short of genuine heroes, Osama bin Laden has emerged as a new cult figure."[16] In Sudan, spiritual leader Hassan Abdallah al-Turabi told a reporter for the *Christian Science Monitor*: "Bin Laden lives in a very remote place, but now—ho, ho,—you [Americans] raised him as the hero, the very symbol of all anti-West forces in the world. All the Arab and Muslim young people, believe me, look to him as an example." Al-Turabi concluded his remarks by saying that the widespread hatred of the United States in the wake of the ill-fated attacks would "create 100,000 bin Ladens."[17]

The missile attack served a further purpose. It strengthened the bonds between al Qaeda and the Taliban. Prior to the bombings, the relationship between bin Laden and Mullah Omar was strained to the limit. Mullah Omar, who was seeking international recognition for his government in Afghanistan, did not appreciate bin Laden's repeated calls for violence against Americans.[18] He declared that the fatwas were "null and void" since bin Laden lacked the religious authority to issue them.[19] The scruffy Taliban regulars resented the arrogance of the Arabs with their refined manners and attitude of condescension toward Pashtun customs and beliefs. Tensions between the two groups became so intense that exchanges of gunfire erupted between Taliban soldiers and bin Laden's bodyguards.[20] In June 1998, the Taliban struck a deal with Saudi officials to send bin Laden to a Saudi prison in exchange for Saudi support and US recognition. According to the *Los Angeles Times*, Prince Turki bin Faisal, head of the Saudi General Intelligence Agency, confided to US officials that it was "a deal done."[21]

Mullah Omar reacted with outrage at both the bombing and the deal. His government was merely honoring the traditional Pashtun code of *milmastia* that demands protection for all Muslims who seek shelter in their country, even if such shelter means risking the safety of all inhabitants. To violate the code would constitute betrayal of a brother and a violation of Islamic teaching. "Extraditing Osama bin Laden," the mullah declared, "is tantamount to leaving a pillar of our religion."[22]

Following the attack, when Prince Turki bin Faisal returned to Afghanistan to renegotiate the surrender of bin Laden to Saudi officials, he found the one-eyed mullah a changed man. "Mullah Omar was very heated," Prince Turki later recalled. "In a loud voice he denounced all our efforts and praised bin Laden as a worthy and legitimate scholar of Islam. He told me we should not do the infidel's work by taking Osama from them."[23]

The opportunity to separate the Taliban from al Qaeda had been lost, and, with it, the possibility of preventing future acts of terror. "Rather than trying to divide and conquer," Dr. Larry Goodson, professor of Middle East studies at the US Army War College, said in the wake of the missile attacks, "we adopted the approach to keep Afghanistan in a box. We were not going to recognize them. We were not going to aid them in significant ways. In fact, we took a very hard line toward the Taliban regime."[24]

In the wake of the attack, money poured into al Qaeda's coffers from Islamic charitable and humanitarian organizations throughout the world. By 1998, the Global Relief Foundation in Chicago, knowingly or unknowingly, began raising more than $5 million a year for bin Laden and his holy war against the United States. Many American "charities" with official tax-exempt status collected millions that would go toward the *jihad* and the destruction of the United States. These charities included the Hatikva Center, the Holy Land Foundation for Relief and Development, the Al-Wafa Humanitarian Organization, and Benevolence International in Chicago.[25] According to the Al-Jazeera news network, the Al-Haramain Islamic Foundation, located in Ashland, Oregon, with prayer houses in Ashland and Springfield, Missouri, raised over $30 million a year—money that would go, in part, to bin Laden for his holy war against Christians and Jews.[26]

Bin Laden continued his search to amass and develop new weapons for his nuclear arsenal. On August 16, 1998, Israeli military intelligence sources reported that bin Laden gave $4 million as a down payment to an arms dealer in Kazakstan, who promised to provide the emir with yet another suitcase bomb. Israel responded to this development by sending a cabinet minister to Kazakstan in order to persuade Kazak officials that emergency measures must be adopted to prevent the sale from taking place.[27]

On September 25, 1998, bin Laden's aide Mamdouh Mahmud Salim was arrested in Munich, Germany, for attempting to buy nuclear materials, including highly enriched uranium.[28]

Al-Jazeera, the Arabian television station, now became the most potent outlet for bin Laden's propaganda. In January 1999, Al-Jazeera broadcast its first profile of bin Laden, in which he spoke about his childhood, his life in exile, his political and religious views, and his intent to make use of nuclear weapons against the United States.[29] It was the closest thing to a talk show appearance that bin Laden had ever done. Throughout the interview, the emir appeared relaxed, authoritative, devout, and ascetic. The show was a great success throughout the Middle East and enhanced bin Laden's image as "the lion of Islam."

By 1999 he had established a well-equipped and fortified weapons factory in Kandahar for development and production of chemical, bacteriological, and nuclear weapons with the help of Pakistani ISI officials.[30] Viruses causing deadly diseases, such as ebola and salmonella, were imported from Russia; botulinum biotoxin was obtained from the Czech Republic; and deadly anthrax from North Korea.[31] At the weapons factory, al Qaeda operatives were trained to grow "lethal biological cultures" that could be used to poison water supplies along with the means of releasing lethal gases in major metropolitan areas.

A second base for the development of weapons of mass destruction was created in Zenica, Bosnia-Herzegovina, where an isolated farmhouse was converted into a "research center" for advanced weaponry.[32] Much of the research was devoted to the creation of human bombs—individuals who could carry and spread an incredibly virulent form of bubonic plague that remains resistant to treatment with chloramphenicol or one of the tetracyclines.

A third such installation was established at Derunta, fifteen miles from Jalalabad. Here, operatives were instructed in the use of ricin, one of the most toxic biological agents on earth.[33] By 2000, over forty laboratories had been established throughout Afghanistan to create weapons of mass destruction for use against the "Great Satan" (bin Laden's preferred moniker for the United States).[34]

While the Taliban persisted in its struggle against the Northern Alliance, bin Laden made preparations for a "night of power" for January 3, 2000, the holiest day of Ramadan, with the bombing of a US warship, USS *The Sullivans*. But al Qaeda's small boat, loaded with boxes of heavy explosives, sank as soon as it was launched, forcing a revision in plans.

The revised plans were activated on October 10, 2000, when USS *Cole* cruised into Aden in Yemen for a short "gas and go" stop. As soon as it was anchored, a skiff packed with five hundred pounds of C-4 plastic explosives slipped from its mooring and sped across the harbor toward the *Cole*. The US soldiers waved at the two suicide bombers who were manning the boat. As soon as the skiff reached the port side of the hull, the terrorists pressed the detonator, blowing a gaping hole in the side of the warship. Seventeen American sailors were killed. The only disappointment for al Qaeda was that the operative who was ordered to video the attack for propaganda purposes fell asleep at his observation point on Steamer Point.[35] None of the al Qaeda operatives were apprehended on their return to Afghanistan. The Clinton administration waved its sword at bin Laden and pledged retaliation. But no retaliation was taken. This lack of action was accepted as another sign of American "weakness," emboldening bin Laden to launch his next attack on American soil.

In February 2001, the United States failed to take advantage of a final opportunity to prevent the attack on 9/11. Senior Taliban leaders again expressed their willingness to exile bin Laden to a third world country in exchange for recognition of their regime as the legitimate government of Afghanistan. Taliban foreign minister Abdul Wakil Muttawakil told the press: "We hope the new American administration will be more flexible and engage with us."[36] But such hopes were in vain. The George W. Bush administration was far more inflexible and far less willing to engage in peaceful resolutions than the Clinton administration. Dick Cheney was a former secretary of defense; Gen. Colin Powell had served as chairman of the Joint Chiefs of Staff; and Donald Rumsfeld had acted as secretary of defense under Gerald Ford. These men stood in the front ranks of the Bush administration. Behind them were individuals who were inclined by nature and experience to take a tough stance against terrorists and terrorist regimes.[37]

The stage was now set and the characters in place for the opening act of Armageddon. What would happen could not be altered. Bin Laden believed it was the will of Allah.

CHAPTER 4

PRESTO

The towers are an economic power and not a children's school. Those that were there are men that supported the biggest economic power in the world. They have to review their books. We will do as they do. If they kill our women and our innocent people, we will kill their women and their innocent people. Not all terrorism is cursed; some is blessed. America and Israel exercise their condemned terrorism. We practice the good terrorism, which stops them from killing our children in Palestine and elsewhere.

—Osama bin Laden, 2002

The enemy in this war is not "terrorism" but militant Islam.
—Eliot Cohen, *Wall Street Journal,*
November 20, 2001

September 11, 2001, represented an attack of amazing precision. At 8:46 AM, American Airlines Flight 11, at the speed of 470 miles per hour, smashed into the north tower of the World Trade Center between the ninety-fourth and ninety-eighth floors.

The Boeing 767-200 had departed from Logan Airport in Boston. It carried ninety-two passengers and ten thousand gallons of jet fuel.

At 9:02 AM, United Airlines Flight 175, at the speed of 586 miles per hour, hit the south tower between the seventy-eighth and eighty-fourth floors. The aircraft, also a Boeing 767-200 from Boston, carried sixty-five passengers and ten thousand gallons of fuel.

The planes did not explode like bombs. A fraction of a second after impact at both towers, fireballs erupted and expanded for several seconds, consuming a small measure of the jet fuel. The rest of the burning fuel swept through the towers. The temperatures within the towers rose to two thousand degrees Fahrenheit. In the northwest corner of the south tower, molten metal flowed like lava down the side of the building.[1]

At 9:40 AM, American Airlines Flight 77 struck the west side of the Pentagon. The Boeing 757 had departed from nearby Dulles Airport with sixty-five passengers. The plane blasted a hole five stories high and two hundred feet wide into the military complex, killing 189, including the passengers and Pentagon personnel.

Only the fourth airplane would fail to reach its appointed destination. At 10:10 AM, United Airlines Flight 93 crashed in a field in Shanksville, Pennsylvania, eighty miles southeast of Pittsburgh, with forty-five passengers aboard. The 757 had been scheduled to depart from Newark Airport at 8:00 AM, but a forty-minute delay put the flight behind schedule and thwarted the plans of the hijackers. Through cell phones, passengers learned of the attacks on the World Trade Center and the Pentagon. A struggle ensued between several of the passengers and the terrorists before the plane went down. The hijackers purportedly had targeted the White House. They had been prevented from successfully completing their mission, however, not by any fault in planning or weakness of resolve but simply by a mere quirk of fate.

The Twin Towers stood as an abomination before the eyes of

bin Laden and the al Qaeda terrorists. They loomed as huge monuments to mammon, vivid representations of Western greed and imperialism, modern-day Towers of Babel that rose as effronteries to the sovereignty of heaven. According to Daniel Pipes, their fall was reportedly greeted by shouts of joy from millions of Muslims in Indonesia, Malaysia, Bangladesh, India, Sri Lanka, Oman, Yemen, Sudan, Bosnia, and the United Kingdom.[2]

At a meeting of top officials of the Bush administration on September 12, Secretary of Defense Donald Rumsfeld asked the key question: "Do we focus on bin Laden and al Qaeda or terrorism more broadly?"

"Start with bin Laden, which [is what] Americans expect," President Bush said. "Then, if we succeed, we've struck a huge blow and can move forward."[3]

Killing or capturing bin Laden became the central objective of the military campaign. This, Rumsfeld believed, could be accomplished only by "draining the swamp of Afghanistan."[4]

The cooperation of Pakistan was deemed to be crucial for the "swamp draining." Pakistan was not only the native land of the Taliban but also a central source of military supplies and new recruits for the struggle against the Northern Alliance. Pakistani president Pervez Musharraf was presented with a tempting carrot—assist the United States in hunting down Bin Laden in exchange for the following: the lifting of the trade restrictions, which would allow up to $426 million in new imports; and a pledge of assistance in the conflict with India over Kashmir. Musharraf, sensing an immediate means to stabilize his country's wobbly economy, agreed, thereby becoming, in the eyes of the *mujahadeen*, "a dead man walking."[5]

On October 7, 2001, President George W. Bush addressed the nation concerning plans for the upcoming war on terror as follows:

> Now this war will not be like the war against Iraq a decade ago,
> with a decisive liberation of territory and a swift conclusion. It

65

will not look like the air war above Kosovo two years ago, where no ground troops were used and not a single American was lost in combat.

Our response involves far more than instant retaliation and isolated strikes. Americans should not expect one battle, but a lengthy campaign unlike any other we have ever seen. It may include dramatic strikes visible on TV and covert operations secret even in success.

We will starve terrorists of funding, turn them against one another, drive them from place to place until there is no refuge or rest.

And we will pursue nations that provide aid or safe haven to terrorism. Every nation in every region now has a decision to make: either you are with us, or you are with the terrorists.

From this day forward, any nation that continues to harbor or support terrorism will be regarded by the United States as a hostile regime. Our nation has been put on notice; we're not immune from attack. We will take defensive measures against terrorism to protect Americans.[6]

On September 23, President Bush held a highly confidential telephone conversation with Russia's president Vladimir Putin. The seventy-minute conversation resulted in an earthshaking shift in the global balance of power that would have a profound impact on bin Laden and the course of the war on terror. Putin gave the nod for US forces to enter Afghanistan and central Asia with tactical nuclear weapons. These weapons, according to the agreement, were to be deployed under the following circumstances:

- If bin Laden first employed nuclear, biological, or chemical weapons against US troops within the Little Pamir and Hindu Kush regions of Afghanistan
- If Taliban fighters used chemical or biological weapons against Pakistan in retaliation for the US invasion

- If Muslim terrorist groups with ties to al Qaeda launched assaults using weapons of mass destruction against US military or civilian targets
- If using nuclear weapons proved to be the only means to prevent heavy American combat casualties

In exchange for his consent, Putin gained Bush's approval of the use of similar nuclear weapons in and around Chechnya. By the end of September, Russian bombers carrying neutron bombs were deployed to military air bases in Stavropol, north of Chechnya, Godowta in Georgia to the south, and northern Osetia, west of the troublesome province.[7]

China's reaction to this development was instantaneous. Tactical nuclear missiles and aircraft capable of carrying nuclear bombs were reportedly transported to bases in the Xinjiang region (formerly Turkestan) of northwest China bordering on the central Asian states and Afghanistan. Long Chinese military convoys thundered down the Krakoram road to the Chinese-Afghan-Pakistani borders. The trucks, according to intelligence sources, also contained equipment for detecting and decontaminating areas that fell under attack with nuclear, chemical, or biological weapons.[8] Chinese officials were clearly aware that the outbreak of nuclear warfare in a neighboring country might have disastrous consequences for Chinese citizens who inhabited bordering towns and villages.

As Americans sat glued to their television sets for the latest word on the war on terror, few were aware that the doomsday card had been played and the world's three great powers—the United States, Russia, and China—were scrambling to get their nuclear weapons in place.

A series of unfortunate mistakes ensued—mistakes that would give rise to mendacities and a flood of disinformation, thereby giving credence to the adage that "truth is the first casualty of war."

The first mistake came with the labeling of the war on terrorism as "Operation Infinite Justice." The label, as it turned out, was politically incorrect and served to offend devout Muslims who believed that only Allah could deliver "infinite justice." In Beirut, Sheikh Afif al-Nabulsi, head of south Lebanon's religious scholars, said that the US antiterrorism campaign should be called "Operation Infinite *Injustice*," because, he contended, the war was intended to establish US control over oil-rich former Soviet Muslim republics in central Asia. A hard-line Iranian newspaper suggested that "Infinite Imperialism" might be more appropriate.[9] In response to such statements, the name was quickly changed to "Operation Enduring Freedom," and President Bush expressed his regrets if he had offended anyone.[10]

The second mistake came with the identification of the Taliban with al Qaeda. On the evening of September 11, 2001, President Bush addressed the nation by saying: "We have to force countries to choose. We will make no distinction between the terrorists who committed these acts and those who harbor them." This statement represented the first expression of the so-called Bush Doctrine—a policy that would commit the United States, with or without allies, to a broad-based, long-term war against terrorism in Islamic countries throughout the world. The Taliban was not al Qaeda, and al Qaeda was not the Taliban. But this distinction was instantly dissolved by executive fiat. Overnight, bin Laden's forces were multiplied tenfold. This new alliance, according to Rohan Gunaratna, a Sri Lanka native and principal investigator of the United Nations' Terrorism Prevention Branch, could have been prevented if the Bush administration had allowed President Musharraf a reasonable amount of time to come to terms with Mullah Omar for the surrender of bin Laden to a peacekeeping force or a neutral country.[11]

A third mistake came with the assumption that al Qaeda, like the thirteenth-century Assassins, represented merely a tiny radical fringe group within Islam—a religious aberration that lacked the general support of the Muslim people. This mistake was a result of wishful thinking, if not a willful and boneheaded denial of accepted facts and findings. At the start of Operation Enduring Freedom, US intelligence agencies knew that al Qaeda was peopled by tens of thousands of militants with ties to hundreds of other Islamic terrorist groups throughout the world. [12] What's more, a classified intelligence survey showed that 95 percent of educated Saudis between the ages of twenty-five and forty-one supported bin Laden's *jihad* against America,[13] and a major Gallup poll showed that a majority of the world's Muslim population possessed an unfavorable opinion of the United States.[14]

A host of additional mistakes were made as soon as the military campaign got underway on October 7, with a salvo of fifty missiles from three US cruisers and a US destroyer in the Arabian Sea. One missile struck one of Mullah Omar's residences in Kandahar, killing his stepfather and his ten-year-old son. Another hit the small village of Kouram, killing one hundred civilians. A third destroyed a mosque and a residential village near Jalalabad.[15]

Along with the bombs, the United States dropped food, medicine, and supplies to towns and villages throughout Afghanistan. This was intended to provide clear and certain proof that the United States was a compassionate friend of the poverty-stricken and war-ridden Afghan people. Since less than 30 percent of the Afghanis are literate, most people couldn't read the messages and labels of greetings and goodwill on the boxes. They simply assumed that the CARE packages they found throughout the countryside were miraculous gifts from Allah.[16]

As soon as the US offensive began, bin Laden appeared on television in Kabul with his favorite sidekick, Ayman al-Zawahiri. Clad in camouflage jackets, the two sat before a campfire with sticks and appeared as though they were foreign boy scouts about to toast some marshmallows. Bin Laden said: "God has blessed a vanguard group of Muslims, the forefront of Islam, to destroy America. May God bless them and allot them a supreme place in heaven."[17]

The war appeared to be going extremely well. On November 9, the United States with its coalition forces gained control of the strategic town of Mazar-i-Sharif. Two days later, Taligan in the south and Herat in the west fell with hardly a shot being fired. On November 12, the coalition forces entered Kabul to cheers from a carefully choreographed crowd of onlookers.[18]

In Kabul, a group of journalists discovered discarded and fire-charred documents within a house in the upscale neighborhood of Wazir Akbar Khan, where the Arabs lived. Several documents contained instructions on how to prepare explosives and chemical weapons from common household goods, including the production of the deadly toxin ricin from castor oil seed. Another document, replete with illustrations, provided formulas for the construction of dirty nuclear bombs. Written in Arabic, German, Urdu, and English, these instructions showed, in part, how the detonation of TNT can compress plutonium into a critical mass, sparking a chain reaction that would lead to a thermonuclear explosion.[19]

The coalition forces pressed on to Jalalabad, where they continued to meet little resistance. The invasion of Afghanistan appeared to be a cakewalk. The only US soldiers injured or killed during the first six weeks of combat were targeted on November 10, when the Taliban managed to shoot down a US helicopter, killing two airmen. The incident occurred in Pakistan near the Dalbandin air base, fifty miles from the Afghan border.[20]

In a Jalabad house, US troops came upon a videotape in which bin Laden spoke with a Saudi sheikh about the 9/11 attack. He told the sheikh that he had surprised even his closest confidants with his masterful plan. "They were overjoyed when the first plane hit the building," bin Laden says with a wry smile, "But I said to them—

be patient. We stayed until four in the morning listening to the news. Everyone was most joyous."[21]

As the coalition forces stared at the peaks of the Spin Ghar, the White Mountains, from the palm trees of Jalalabad, the end to the struggle appeared to be in sight. It appeared in the form of the highest peak, Tora Bora, where they believed bin Laden and his cohort of terrorists had disappeared into an impregnable fortress.

The story of the impregnable fortress was purportedly based on testimony to CIA and FBI officials from Viktor Kutsenko, a former Soviet army commander who had served in Afghanistan during the 1980s.[22] The fortress, Kutsenko allegedly claimed, was built 350 yards beneath solid rock near the highest peak of Tora Bora. Others embellished on Kutsenko's testimony so that intelligence sources were able to provide the military with detailed drawings of al Qaeda's mountain lair. The drawings show an intricate underground complex containing a bakery, a hospital with ultrasound equipment, a hotel for two thousand occupants, a mosque, a hydroelectric plant, a library, an arsenal of weapons of mass destruction, and a service bay for several Soviet tanks. US officials believed that a masterful ventilation system had been designed by bin Laden and his engineers to circulate fresh air throughout the structure.[23]

News of the lair was published in the *New York Times* on November 26.[24] On December 2, Secretary of Defense Donald Rumsfeld appeared on *Meet the Press* to assure the American people of the existence of the incredibly elaborate complex within Tora Bora. "And there's not one of those," Rumsfeld told Tim Russert. "There are many of those. And they have been used very effectively. And I might add, Afghanistan is not the only country that has gone underground. Any number of countries have gone underground."

But the modern troglodyte lair did not exist. It was apparently the figment of some overactive imaginations but had become accepted as an indisputable fact by US intelligence agencies.

American B-52 bombers now began to pound the mountainside with "bunker blasters" in a Herculean effort to collapse bin Laden's mythical underground kingdom with its hotel, its hydroelectric plant, and its imaginary arsenal of weapons. On the ground, members of the US Special Forces—Delta Force and Navy SEALs—guided bombs with laser devices to their targets by outlining the mouths of caves that might serve as possible sources of ventilation for the fanciful fortress.[25]

Believing that between sixteen hundred and two thousand of al Qaeda's fiercest fighters were sequestered in the secret lair, Gen. Tommy Franks, who was running the US military campaign from Central Command in Florida, decided that it was much too risky to place US soldiers on the ground. High casualties appeared to be a certainty, and the Bush administration didn't want hundreds of troops returning to the country in body bags.

Flush with over a billion dollars for extra funding, the CIA began to recruit the help of local warlords to join the Northern Alliance in storming the mountain fortress.[26] The US troops, for the most part, merely stood by to take part in the cleanup campaign. The United States, unbeknownst to the American people, was hiring an army of mercenaries to fight its righteous war and preparing them to serve as canon fodder. The situation was becoming increasingly surreal.

As soon as the ground offensive began on December 3, the warlords reported that al Qaeda and Taliban forces were offering fierce resistance. US military officials accepted this report as an indication that bin Laden was holed up in Tora Bora with sixteen hundred to two thousand of his most highly trained soldiers. Indeed, US intelligence officers even reported hearing over short-range radio the ghostly voice of the emir giving orders to his top lieutenants from his lair within the belly of the mountain.[27]

Along with the artillery fire, the United States continued to pound the mountain to smithereens with heavy air strikes. At one point, a so-called daisy cutter—a 6,800-kilogram bomb, the largest conventional weapon in the US arsenal—was dropped on a strategic Tora Bora target.[28] Gen. Richard Myers, chairman of the US Joint Chiefs of Staff, said: "We think we know in general where bin Laden and some of his senior leadership are hiding. We think it's in this so-called Tora Bora area, and that's why we're focusing so hard on the area right now."[29]

By December 11, US officials reported that the caves and mountainside of Tora Bora were littered with the bodies of hundreds of al Qaeda warriors and that the al Qaeda defenses were finally beginning to crumble.[30] In a gesture of goodwill, coalition forces reportedly offered the trapped terrorists a chance to surrender. The offer, according to US officials, was turned down and "fierce fighting" was again reported to have erupted throughout the steep mountainside. The warlords required more supplies, more equipment, more recruits, and more money. Such requests were met without question or complaint. Gen. Tommy Franks now reported that al Qaeda and the Taliban were placed between "a hammer and an anvil."[31] Yet when newsmen traveled to the front lines, they heard no sounds of gunfire and no signs of enemy resistance.[32]

When a final surrender was reached and the last cave breached, the al Qaeda body count, according to the warlords, was estimated to be between two and three hundred, and hundreds more were reported to have been taken as prisoners. As proof of the success of the campaign, the warlords paraded nineteen emaciated and toothless captives before the international press in Kandahar.[33] If the original calculations of between sixteen hundred and two thousand al Qaeda fighters were accurate, then fifteen hundred to seventeen hundred, including bin Laden and al-Zawahiri, must have escaped either eastward to Pakistan or southward to the equally mountainous Paktia section of Afghanistan.[34]

Before the invasion, US officials had instructed President Musharraf to seal the one-hundred-mile border of lawless countryside between Pakistan and Afghanistan with his troops. But the instructions went unheeded. No effective siege of Tora Bora could take place because the back door had been left wide open for bin Laden and his cohorts.[35] "The border with Pakistan was the key," admitted Pir Baksh Bardiwal, the intelligence chief for the Northern Alliance, "but the Americans paid no attention to it. Al Qaeda escaped right out from under their noses."[36]

The best opportunity to capture bin Laden had been lost because of caution. On December 27, a gaunt and gray bin Laden, like the ghost of Christmas Past, appeared on the Al-Jazeera television station with the following message:

> Three months after the blessed strike against world infidelity, namely, America, and two months after the fierce crusade against Islam, it gives us pleasure to speak about the ramifications of these events. These events have revealed extremely important things to Muslims. It has become clear that the West in general, led by America, bears an unspeakable crusader grudge against Islam. Those who lived these months under the continuous bombardments by the various kinds of US aircraft are well aware of this. Many villagers were wiped out without any guilt. Millions of people were expelled during this very cold weather—the oppressed ones of men, women and children.[37]

The US troops entered the "swamp" of Afghanistan, but they had not been able to drain it. Instead, they became bogged down in the treacherous terrain, much like the Soviets before them. Blunders begot more blunders, as the war effort continued to be directed from Command Headquarters in Florida. Millions were squandered on the services of the warlords, who remained loyal neither to the Taliban nor to the Northern Alliance, and a massive military campaign was launched against a target that did not exist. US troops would now fall prey to guerilla attacks and terrorist reprisals that would occur with increasing frequency and ferocity. As phase one of Operation Enduring Freedom came to a close, the nuclear card had been played—with tactical nukes deployed to Afghanistan and the borders of Chechnya—and the stakes for radical Islam would become raised to the limit.

As they combed the tunnels near a former al Qaeda base in Kandahar, US troops made an important discovery: low-grade uranium-238 in a lead-lined canister. Although not weapons grade and unsuitable for use in the construction of a fission bomb, the uranium in the canister could be combined with conventional explosives to make a "dirty nuke"—a nuke that could spread contamination over a wide metropolitan area. This discovery along with the documents found in the house in Kabul convinced military intelligence officials that bin Laden did possess an unknown quantity of dirty nukes. The fact that retreating al Qaeda fighters would leave behind such valuable nuclear material—worth several million on the black market—increased speculation that the terrorists must have taken their "crown jewels" with them.

This conviction that bin Laden possessed dirty nukes was fortified by a confidential report from British intelligence that told of two special agents who, in 2001, managed to infiltrate an al Qaeda training camp in Afghanistan by posing as recruits from a London mosque. After spending weeks learning how to fire Kalishnikov rifles, how to pick planes out of the sky with Stingers and other surface-to-air missiles, and how to pack plastic explosives in a Samsonite suitcase, they were obliged to take the *bayat* (oath of allegiance) to Osama bin Laden—a rite that involved fasting, self-castigation with a whip made of small chains, and days of indoctrination. Upon acceptance into bin Laden's fold, the agents were sent to the city of Herat in western Afghanistan for special operations training. In Herat, they visited an al Qaeda laboratory where scientists and technicians were busy putting the finishing touches on a nuclear weapon they had manufactured from radioactive isotopes. This weapon, let alone any other that had been produced by the terrorist organization, has never been recovered.[38]

On February 11, 2003, an audio message from Osama bin Laden to the people of Iraq was broadcast on the Arab television station Al-Jazeera. In the sixteen-minute message, the world's "most wanted" man provided his own take on the "great battle" of Tora Bora:

> We were about three hundred *mujahadeen*. We dug trenches that were spread in an area that does not exceed one square mile, one trench for every three brothers, so as to avoid the huge human losses resulting from the bombardment.
>
> Since the first hour of the US campaign on 20 Rajab 1422, corresponding to October 7, 2001, our centers were exposed to constant bombardment. And this bombardment continued until mid-Ramadan.
>
> On 17 Ramadan, a very fierce bombardment began, particularly after the US command was informed that some of al Qaeda's leaders were still in Tora Bora, including the humble servant to God [referring to himself] and the brother *mujahad* Dr. Ayman al-Zawahiri.
>
> The bombardment was round-the-clock and the warplanes continued to fly over us day and night. The US Pentagon, together with its allies, worked full-time on blowing up and destroying this small spot, as well as removing it entirely. Planes poured their lava on us, particularly after accomplishing their main mission in Afghanistan.
>
> The US forces attacked us with smart bombs, bombs that weigh thousands of pounds, cluster bombs, and bunker busters. Bombers, like the B-52, used to fly overhead for more than two

hours and drop between twenty and thirty bombs at a time. The modified C-130 aircraft kept carpet-bombing us at night, using modern types of bombs.

The US dared not break into our positions, despite the unprecedented massive bombing and terrible propaganda targeting this completely besieged small area. This is in addition to the forces of hypocrites, whom they prodded to fight us for fifteen days nonstop. Every time they attacked us, we forced them out of our area carrying their dead and wounded. Is there any clearer evidence of their cowardice, fear, and lies regarding their legends about their alleged power?

To sum it up, the battle resulted in the complete failure of the international alliance of evil, with all its forces, to overcome a small number of *mujahadeen*—three hundred *mujahadeen*—hunkered down in trenches spread over an area of one square mile under a temperature of minus ten degrees Celsius.

The battle resulted in the injury of 6 percent of personnel— we hope God will accept them as martyrs—and the damage of 2 percent of the trenches, praise be to God.

If all the world forces of evil could not achieve their goals on a one square mile of area against a small number of *mujahadeen* with very limited capabilities, how can these evil forces triumph over the Muslim world? This is impossible, God willing, if people adhere to their religion and insist on *jihad* for its sake.

CHAPTER 5

THE MYSTERY OF SHAH-I-KOT

So the only master of the world wants to threaten us, but make no mistake: Afghanistan, as it was in the past—the Great Britain, he came, the Red Army, he came—Afghanistan is a swamp. People who enter here laughing are exiting injured.
— Mullah Abdul Salam Zaif,
former Taliban ambassador to Pakistan

When you're wounded and left on Afghanistan's plains,
And the women come up to cut up what remains,
Jest roll to your rifle and blow out your brains,
An' go to your Gawd like a soldier.
— Rudyard Kipling, "The Young British Soldier"

At the start of "Operation Anaconda," the code name for the spring offensive against al Qaeda and the Taliban, US officials paid little heed to the harsh lessons of Afghan history. From the mid-nineteenth century to the close of the twentieth century, the world's superpowers of the time had tried to occupy and subdue the unruly Afghans with horrific results. In January 1842, Afghan

79

tribesmen mowed down 16,500 British troops under Eton-educated officers. Dr. William Brydon, a British medic, was the sole survivor. Rudyard Kipling immortalized the conflict with the following lines from "Arithmetic on the Frontier":

A scrimmage in a border station,
A canter down some dark defile,
Two thousand pounds of education
Drops to a ten-rupee jezail.
The crammer's boast, the squadron's pride,
Shot like a rabbit in a ride.[1]

Two more British invasions were to follow, leaving a British secretary of state to sum up the failed attempts to colonize the country by writing: "All that has been accomplished has been the disintegration of the state which it was desired to see strong, friendly, and independent. There is a condition of anarchy throughout the remainder of the country."[2]

In 1979, eighty-five thousand Soviet troops invaded Afghanistan in an effort to prop up the puppet regime of Babrak Karmal. The invasion prompted seven Afghan warlords to set aside their disputes in order to form the *mujahadeen*—the "warriors of God." The alliance gained financial support and a steady supply of recruits from Pakistan and Saudi Arabia. The United States joined the struggle when President Jimmy Carter came up with $30 million in covert aid for the *mujahadeen* to check the spread of communism.[3] This amount was greatly increased under the Reagan administration. By 1984, over $250 million a year in arms and equipment was being sent to Afghanistan to bolster the resistance. By 1988, the *mujahadeen* were receiving $700 million a year from Uncle Sam. By this time, the Reagan administration was obliged to ship Tennessee mules to Afghanistan so that the weapons could be hauled to remote rebel outposts in the mountains on a regular basis.[4]

With the increase in aid came an increase in carnage. The *muja-hadeen* were now able to pick off Soviet planes, tanks, and military bases with thousands of US-supplied Stingers and other surface-to-air rockets. By the time the conflict came to an end in 1989, between fifteen thousand and thirty thousand Soviet soldiers had been killed in action, thousands more by disease, and hundreds of thousands had been wounded. The might of the great Red Army had been vanquished by an alliance of third world tribesmen. "The lesson here is that *jihad* is a duty," bin Laden, who had fought in the struggle, had said. "We believe that those who waged *jihad* in Afghanistan performed a great duty. They managed, with their limited resources of RPGs, antitank mines, and Kalishnikovs, to defeat the biggest legend known to mankind, to destroy the biggest war machine, and to remove from our minds the so-called 'big powers.'"[5]

Operation Anaconda was launched on a bit of disinformation. In January 2002, Badshah Khan Zadran, an Afghan warlord on the US payroll, purportedly told CIA officials that thousands of al Qaeda and Taliban soldiers were regrouping in the mountainous region of Shah-i-Kot in preparation to strike US military bases and to topple the interim Afghan government of Hamid Karzai.[6] This claim appeared to be verified by a series of photographs from an aerial reconnaissance vehicle called the Predator. The photographs, taken from an altitude of twenty-six thousand feet, showed two tall, thin, and bearded men in *shalwart kameez* (the loose-fitting tunics and baggy pants of al Qaeda and Taliban soldiers) standing before a tarpaulin at the entrance to a cave. US military officials assumed that the tarpaulin was covering a machine-gun post and that the men, because of their height, dress, and posture, were Arabs and therefore al Qaeda operatives.[7]

Khan's information should have been received with suspicion. On December 20, 2001, he reportedly triggered an attack on a convoy of Paktia elders that left sixty-five dead. The elders were aligned to neither bin Laden nor Mullah Omar. They were purportedly Khan's political rivals who had resisted his attempts to add Gardez, the central city of Paktia, to his fiefdom.[8]

The plans for Operation Anaconda called for the coalition forces to encircle the al Qaeda and Taliban forces like a huge snake, hence the name, in order to squeeze the life out of them. Fifteen hundred soldiers, including special forces from Australia, Canada, Germany, Denmark, France, and Norway, along with American and Afghan troops, were to form the vanguard of the assault by heading southward from Gardez, then sweeping east toward the Shah-i-Kot valley, while pushing the terrorist forces before them. To seal the escape route to Pakistan that had been left open during the shelling of Tora Bora, US troops from the 101st Airborne were stationed along the mountainous ridges of the Afghan-Pakistan border to the north, east, and south.

As conceived by the Pentagon, the coil of the anaconda would become a vast ring that would encompass seventy-two square miles and reach an altitude of twelve thousand feet. Once the enemy became squeezed and entrapped within this coil, US forces would unleash their full firepower to blast the terrorists to kingdom come.[9]

Things did not follow as planned. As soon as the operation got underway, coalition forces complained that they were being met with unexpected, heavy resistance. One American soldier was killed along with four members of the Northern Alliance. The fighting appeared to be fiercest at Operation Position Ginger, where troops of the Tenth Mountain Division were bogged down in the mud for more than forty-eight hours. The intelligence reports appeared to be wrong. Instead of a few hundred al Qaeda forces, US military officials now estimated that more than two thousand enemy forces had gathered to launch a massive counteroffensive.

The coalition land forces summoned air support, and within the first twenty-four hours more than two hundred bombs, including a two-thousand-pound "thermobaric bomb," were dropped at Position Ginger. The US military commanders gradually became convinced that the advance units inadvertently had stumbled into a hornet's nest, the last stronghold of enemy resistance.

The situation didn't make sense. How could two of the "most wanted groups" in the world—the Taliban and al Qaeda—wander around a war zone and set up shop within twenty miles of Gardez, a busy provincial city, under the nose of the most sophisticated military intelligence unit in the world?[10]

During the second day of battle, seven Americans were killed when enemy marksmen downed a Chinook—a US assault helicopter—with their rifles. A senior air force commander confided to the press: "The way we lost those seven guys was a repeat of Somalia."[11] In this way, he conjured up the image of the disastrous battle of Mogadishu in 1993 when a Black Hawk helicopter was downed and eighteen American soldiers were killed—an incident that became known in military circles as "our other Vietnam."[12]

By the sixth day, White House officials claimed that the enemy was being systematically decimated and that more than eight hundred enemy bodies lay strewn throughout the mountainous terrain of Position Ginger.[13] Commenting on the high number of enemy casualties, Secretary Rumsfeld said that he didn't want to get into the "numbers game" but could say with certainty that "hundreds" of al Qaeda and Taliban soldiers had been killed during the opening days of the conflict.[14] Similarly, Maj. Gen. Frank Hagenbeck, commander of the Coalition Joint Task Force, said that "hundreds" were "confirmed dead," although the actual number could not be stated "because of the types of killing that went on—with laser-guided bombs, for example."[15] Throughout the operation, the enemy death toll, as a reporter for the *New York Times* pointed out, came to rise and fall like "the fluctuations of a troubled currency: 100, 500, 200, 800, 300."[16]

As the battle of Shah-i-Kot raged, megaton bombs were dropped at the increased rate of 260 a day. On March 8, President Bush said: "These people evidently don't want to give up, and that's okay. If that's their attitude, we'll just have to adjust, and they'll have made a mistake."[17]

The tenaciousness of the enemy amid the constant bombings and heavy artillery attacks led several US military officials to believe that Mullah Omar and bin Laden must be concealed in a bunker or cave and that the terrorists were fighting to the last man in order to defend them.[18]

It took ten days of fierce fighting for the Americans to gain the upper hand. By that time, the coalition forces reported that eleven soldiers had been killed, eight of them American, and eighty-eight wounded. In the Pentagon there was a growing sense of euphoria that a monumental battle had been won and that the tide of the war had been turned.

When the fighting came to an end on March 12, Gen. Tommy Franks hailed Operation Anaconda as "an unqualified and absolute success."[19] Major General Hagenbeck added: "The world is a safer place than it was on the second of March when we inserted several thousand coalition forces—including soldiers, sailors, airmen and marines—that put their lives on the line to confront al Qaeda and Taliban terrorists."[20]

Following the operation, a force of seven hundred US and Canadian soldiers searched more than thirty caves in Shah-i-Kot and collected papers, weapons, ammunition, and other items left behind by the enemy. They also discovered computer records to add to the intelligence picture of international terrorism and personal diaries kept by some fighters detailing ways of countering US high-tech weapons and of disabling attack helicopters with well-placed shots from Kalishnikov automatic rifles.[21]

On March 18, the last day of maneuvers, the coalition military commanders were faced with a bewildering mystery. The resistance had been fierce. Hundreds of enemy solders had been "confirmed" dead. The escape route to Pakistan had been sealed. And yet only ten enemy soldiers were taken prisoner, and fewer than twenty bodies were found within the battle zone. "There were no dead al Qaeda fighters," a *USA Today* journalist reported from eastern Afghanistan. "There were no fresh graves. Just one macabre reminder stuck out: dried blood on a patch of dirt here in the village."[22]

The absence of corpses and the scant number of prisoners gave rise to the speculation that the fighters had escaped before the launching of the full military offensive on March 2; that the spotting of the bodies had been either hype, hallucination, or wishful thinking; and that the 3,250 bombs may have been dropped on largely uninhabited territory.[23] Interrogation of the few al Qaeda captives confirmed the suspicion that bin Laden had been in a warren of caves burrowed in the mountain at Position Ginger and that corrupt Afghan militias in the employ of the coalition forces managed to arrange his escape. Gen. Tommy Franks now became the brunt of widespread criticism, with the British press stating that his reliance on Afghan warlords with ambiguous loyalties represented "the greatest error in the war."[24]

The British forces now came to the fore of the war effort, as seventeen hundred Royal Marines from the 45 Commandos arrived at the US military base in Bagram. The US Central Command had issued a call for help to British prime minister Tony Blair at the end of March after coming to the realization that Operation Anaconda had gone hopelessly awry. Blair responded with the largest deployment of British troops since the 1991 Gulf War. The prime minister expressed his belief that the campaign would be bloody and "twenty or more" Marines might be killed in the struggle.[25]

The Royal Marines, under the command of Brig. Gen. Roger Lane, represented an elite unit that had been trained for months in

Norway for mountain warfare. They claimed to possess the stamina and the skills for guerilla operations at high altitudes that American infantrymen failed to display. "The Yanks are great with all the bells and whistles and logistics, but in terms of boots on the ground, they don't have the experience that we do," a young British Marine said upon arrival at Camp Gibraltar.[26]

The British operation got underway on April 13. It was dubbed "Operation Ptarmigan" after a tough bird with feathered toes that lives in Alaska. The ptarmigan is known to be fiercely territorial and wards off all intruders with aerial assaults and a variety of croaking, gargling, and screaming sounds.[27]

Apart from releasing the code name of the operation, the Brits failed to inform US Central Command of any details regarding their plans to ferret out the estimated two thousand bin Laden fighters who reportedly remained in the Paktia region. Gen. Tommy Franks learned that Ptarmigan was underway only after watching a CNN news bulletin that was aired twenty hours after the operation was launched.[28] The bulletin included an interview with Brigadier General Lane, who expressed great confidence in the skill of his Marines and predicted that the war would be over in a matter of weeks.

Lane's prediction proved false. The grandiose operation named after a troublesome grouse never took flight. It simply laid an egg. Instead of acquiescing to the British army's desire for a military confrontation in the mountains, the al Qaeda forces simply melted away within the North-West Frontier Province of Pakistan. On April 18, five days after setting out with bagpipes and braggadocio, the British Marines returned to the military base at Bagram without firing a single shot or spotting a single enemy soldier. At a press conference, Lt. Col. Tim Chicken said: "Whilst we did not come across any Taliban or al Qaeda, there was evidence and indications that the facilities [the caves in the mountains] had been used."[29] Chicken maintained that the mission was not a complete failure since the Marines had managed to confiscate and destroy a large cache of weapons. The lieutenant colonel, as it turned out, misspoke. The weapons proved to be the property of a warlord in the employ of the CIA.[30] The warlord expressed outrage and demanded full compensation for his loss from the coalition forces.

The Brits refused to give up the effort. On May 2, Operation Ptarmigan transmogrified into Operation Snipe as one thousand commandos were sent to comb a remote area of the Afghan mountains at an altitude of fourteen hundred feet for the elusive enemy. But no trace of al Qaeda or Taliban forces could be found, and the search ended on May 11.

On May 17, Operation Snipe gave way to Operation Condor as the Royal Marines combed the mountains of southeast Afghanistan only to encounter a few friendly villagers. The operation came to a swift and unceremonious conclusion on May 22.

The Royal Marines remained steadfast, as Operation Condor became Operation Buzzard on May 29. The commandos now were dispatched to comb every nook and cranny throughout the Kowst region for a sign of the enemy. No sign was to be found.

Trying to put a positive spin on the military initiatives, Brigadier General Lane said that his troops had dealt a "significant blow" to the enemy and that not spotting a single Taliban or al Qaeda soldier was "from a strategic point of view, an encouraging sign."[31] The British press didn't buy it and began running headlines about the high command keeping the truth from the home front and the Royal Marines losing the enemy in thin air.

On July 9, the last of the British operations came to a close. By that time, the most dangerous enemy that the commandos encountered was a strange viral disorder known as "Winter Vomiting Disease" that landed 28 of the elite corps in the 34 Field Hospital and 340 in quarantine.[32]

As the summer heat bore down on the plains of Afghanistan

with temperatures reaching 110 degrees, the coalition forces, at last, came to the clear and certain conclusion that the stronghold of al Qaeda and the Taliban was neither in Tora Bora nor Shah-i-Kot nor any other place within Afghanistan. It was located across the rugged border in the North-West Frontier Province of Pakistan, an area that had been created in 1901 by the British, who could never manage to subdue and "civilize" the many tribes and clans who inhabited it.

One of the most treacherous and forbidding places on the planet—a place where parched deserts (where summer temperatures reach 124 degrees Fahrenheit) give way to snow-capped mountains (with peaks topping 15,000 feet), the North-West Frontier Province remains the land of *badal*, or "revenge," where a man may be killed for an idle word or a wayward glance. It is a land unto itself—free from taxes, foreign dignitaries, cable television, and any semblance of law and order. The jurisdiction of the Pakistani police and military ends one hundred yards off any road leading to its towns and villages.

Bin Laden was there with Mullah Omar and his top lieutenants, including Ayman al-Zawahiri, a.k.a. the Doctor, safe and somewhat secure from President Bush, Prime Minister Blair, and President Musharraf, among the thousands of radical Muslim fundamentalists who swarmed around the hundreds of *madrassahs* that lined the countryside. It represented ostensibly "friendly" territory that could not be invaded without sparking an international incident and cries from thousands of minarets throughout the world.

Two pressing questions faced US intelligence officials: What the hell was bin Laden doing there? And what were his plans for the next attack against the country he called "the Great Satan"?

Some answers came with the arrest of Khalid Shaikh Mohammed, al Qaeda's military operations chief, in Karachi, Pakistan, on March 2, 2003, the launch date for Operation Anaconda.

After days of interrogations, the terrorist chief admitted that bin Laden's goal was to create a "nuclear hell storm" like the 1945 blast in Hiroshima that killed 140,000 Japanese. Unlike other attacks that could be planned and conducted by lower-level al Qaeda leaders, the terrorist chief said, the chain of command for the nuclear operation answered directly to bin Laden, al-Zawahiri, and a mysterious scientist called "Dr. X."[33]

Through further interrogation of Khalid Shaikh, coupled with information retrieved from his laptop computer, US intelligence officials learned of an impending plot to explode dirty nukes on American soil. Four purported al Qaeda operatives—Adrian El Shukrijumah, Anas al-Liby, Jaber A. Elbaneh, and Amer El-Maati—had been sent to Hamilton, Ontario, where they either enrolled or posed as students at McMaster University, a state-of-the-art technological institution that housed a five-megawatt nuclear research reactor. The task of the four sleeper agents was to buy or steal radioactive material through students, technicians, or teachers who had access to the research reactor or to radioactive medical waste for the purpose of constructing dirty nukes on American soil.[34]

Jane Johnson, a spokesperson for McMaster University, declined to comment on whether El Shukrijumah and the other agents were ever students at the school. She insisted that such information was confidential.[35]

William H. Parrish, an official with the Department of Homeland Security, said that the four agents intended to spearhead a nuclear attack that was to occur simultaneously at various locations throughout the United States.[36]

The four men escaped arrest. Intelligence officials believe they may have returned to the Middle East.[37]

PART TWO

THE REAL NEWS

Praise be to God. Praise be to God, who says: "O Prophet, strive hard against the unbelievers and hypocrites and be firm against them. Their abode is hell—an evil refuge, indeed." May God's blessings be upon our prophet Muhammad, who says: "He who is killed in defense of his property is a martyr; he who is killed in self-defense is a martyr; he who is killed in defense of his religion is a martyr; and he who is killed in defense of his family is a martyr." I tell you the American people: God willing, we will continue to fight you. We will continue the martyrdom operations inside and outside the United States until you end your injustice, abandon your stupidity, and curb your insolent fellows. You should know that we count our killed ones, may God have mercy on their souls, particularly those killed in Palestine at the hands of your allies, the Jews. So, we will punish you for them, God willing, just like what happened on the New York day. Just remember what I told you at the time about our security and your security. . . . We fight those who fight us and chop off their heads with our swords. There is no peace until infidelity is defeated. God suffices us, and he is our supporter, and you do not have any supporter.

—Osama bin Laden, broadcast on Al-Jazeera,
October 18, 2003

CHAPTER 6

IN THE BELLY OF THE BEAST

You who believe! Take not the Jews and the Christians for your friends and protectors: they are but friends and protectors to each other. And he among you who turns to them in friendship is one of them.

—Koran 5:14

Against them make ready your strength to the utmost of your power, including steeds of war, to strike terror into the hearts of the enemies of Allah. Whatever you spend in the cause of Allah shall be repaid to you and you shall not be treated unjustly.

—Koran 8:60

The annual four-day Soldier of Fortune Exposition, held in mid-September, is a unique event. After enrolling at a registration desk in a resort casino, participants board buses to venture into the Nevada desert (120 miles from the heart of Las Vegas), where they fire machine guns at junk cars and trucks, engage in pugil-stick combat with instructors disguised as members of the *mujahadeen*, and participate in night maneuvers with paint-ball guns and with rubber knifes caked with red dye that leave "cuts" on the skin of enemy opponents.

The expo also offers more restful and cerebral activities, including seminars on the constitutional right of all Americans to join a local militia and install rocket launchers on their lawns, along with crash courses in such subjects as anatomy (the parts of the body that represent instant "kill" areas), physics (the trajectory paths of high-velocity bullets), botany (edible plants and roots for guerilla warriors), and chemistry (formulas for handmade bombs from common kitchen ingredients).

Hundreds of vendors offer a highly unique assortment of goods and gifts: Nazi marching CDs, leather vests and briefs, camouflage suits, videos of "biker bitches" firing machine guns at cardboard male targets, fashionable field glasses, infrared telescopes, mess kits with Teflon cooking utensils, food items (including a wide variety of beef jerky), jewelry (dog tags, identification bracelets, handcuffs), headgear (helmets, military caps, red and green berets), and thousands of guns from hundreds of manufacturers—Heckler & Koch self-loading pistols, double-action Mausers, Walther military pistols, selective-fire Berettas, AMT Hardballers, Colt Pythons and King Cobras, Webley pocket pistols, Smith and Wesson service revolvers, Uzis, double-action Spectres, BMX weapons that can be used as submachine guns or grenade launchers, M16s, Vietcong K-50Ms, Giat sniping rifles, and Browning antitank machine guns.

Those who make the right connection can purchase an unregistered Saturday night special—a .38 Harrington and Richardson for three hundred dollars—or the AK-47 of your dreams (with no vend number) for five thousand dollars from the trunks of vehicles in the parking lot.

And it is here—not within the offices of the Pentagon or the Department of Homeland Security—where one can obtain firsthand information about bin Laden, the regrouping of the Taliban, and the plans of al Qaeda for the next 9/11.

Such information, albeit not all of equal accuracy, comes from some of the mercenaries who meander through the crowds of gun geeks and rednecks in perfectly tailored and impeccably pressed Armani suits. They are middle-aged (between forty and fifty) with ramrod-straight comportment and barely an ounce of fat on their bodies. Many have served in such places as El Salvador, Nicaragua, Bosnia, and Albania. They come to the convention not to fire machine guns or to participate in the candy-ass maneuvers. They are here to seek contracts with military corporations from Australia, South Africa, England, and Alexandria, Virginia. Some are former Green Berets, SEALs, and Rangers. The standard fee for their services is fifteen thousand dollars a month plus expenses.

These unsmiling and mysterious figures do not present themselves as soldiers for hire, "mercs," or paid assassins. They call themselves "repairmen." There is a good reason for the subterfuge. Any US citizen who enlists in a foreign army without written approval from both the secretary of defense and the secretary of state must forfeit his US citizenship. The Geneva Convention, in a 1979 protocol, stripped captured mercenaries of the title and protection of POW and sanctioned their execution without appeal to an international court of law as war criminals.[1] In 1989 the United Nations drafted the International Convention against the Recruitment, Use, Financing, and Training of Mercenaries that called upon states to extradite or prosecute any mercenaries found within their borders. By 1980, individual soldiers of fortune no longer were permitted to travel from place to place like modern-day Paladins with guns for hire.

The mercenary business was compelled to undergo a radical transformation. Overnight, private military corporations, such as Sandline, Executive Outcomes, and Military Professional Resources, popped up to offer the services of "repairmen" to international oil companies who sought protection for their oil fields and natural gas assets in Africa and the Middle East from the *muja-*

hadeen. The military corporations also offered the services of "repairmen" to emerging third world countries (Colombia, Angola, Congo, and Papua New Guinea) who wanted to safeguard natural resources such as diamonds, gold, and uranium from bandits and warlords.[2] The representatives of these military corporations travel to Las Vegas every year to recruit available "repairmen" as independent contractors.

One such repairman at the 2003 expo was Bill Reed (not his real name). He was forty-two with a weathered face, steel gray eyes behind Ray-Bans, closely cropped hair, and a neatly manicured black mustache. He had recently returned from a trip to Pakistan for a military organization in Pretoria, South Africa. His objective was to purchase weapons for that military organization. The weapons were to be used for covert operations in Angola and Sierra Leone. Due to the existing UN arms embargo, the weapons that Reed acquired had to be transferred by rogue Pakistani Intelligence (ISI) officers to Islamabad, where they would be packed in cartons, labeled as construction parts, transported by truck to the port city of Karachi, and shipped on Arab freighters to Freetown.

For the trip, Reed was trained in correct protocol for dealing with the *mujahadeen,* including agents of al Qaeda. Indeed, only by adhering to the protocol could any Westerner hope to emerge alive from the gun factories and weapon bazaars of the North-West Frontier Province.

1. Do not make sexual remarks about women or tell an off-color joke. Maintain a sober and serious manner. Speak only when necessary.
2. Make no flippant mention of religion. Above all, do not smile or appear flippant when mentioning the Koran or the name of the Prophet.
3. When anyone mentions the name or the title of the Prophet

Muhammad, the servant and messenger of Allah, you must cry out the invocation *"Salla-Liahu alaihi wasalam"* ("May Allah bless him and give him peace") or the equally valid *"Alaihi-s-salam"* ("Peace be with him"). Failure to show such reverence could result, at best, in a severe flogging or, at worst, should you be considered an apostate or blasphemer, in the removal of your tongue.

4. Do not wear anything that has Jewish or Christian significance, such as a cross or the Star of David. Anyone who wanders among Muslim tribes sporting such things could be beheaded.

5. Do not squeeze hands when shaking them. Tightening your grip around an outstretched hand is an act of aggression. After shaking hands, touch your chest as a gesture of submission and respect.

6. Never touch an agent of al Qaeda or a member of any other Islamic terrorist group with your left hand. The Muslims wash their privates and wipe their backsides with this hand. It is deemed unclean.

7. Never pass food with your left hand. Such a disrespectful act committed in the presence of certain emirs could result in amputation.

8. Never urinate in the presence of Muslim fundamentalists. This, too, is a sign of disrespect. Always sit or squat when emptying your bladder.

9. Never blow your nose in the presence of people who live by a strict interpretation of Islamic law. Such an act is a grievous insult.

10. Never eat while walking around—not even a candy bar. This is a sign of inhospitality and disrespect.

11. Never take photographs without permission. Above all, never take pictures of women, the infirm, or the elderly.

12. Never gaze at a woman, not even in passing. When a woman, even one dressed in full burqa, appears before you, cast your eyes to the ground.

13. Avoid gazing at another man, even in passing. A Muslim terrorist might assume you are gay, and all homosexuals are an abomination before Allah.

14. Never express admiration for any object belonging to a terrorist. This will compel the terrorist to give the object to you as a gesture of hospitality. He will only be able to reclaim the object by your demise.

15. Never drink alcoholic beverages in any Islamic country or express thirst for a beer while crossing the desert. This shows disrespect for the teachings of the Prophet.

16. Avoid pointing your toes at a host. Such an action implies a threat.

17. Never wear your shoes in a Muslim shrine. If invited to the hut or tent of a member of the *mujahadeen*, immediately remove your shoes at the entranceway.

18. Never violate the Holy Day of Friday by loud and impious behavior.

19. Never carry religious tracts or objects of religious devotion (such as a rosary or a prayer book). Such things will imply that you intend to proselytize the Christian faith.

20. Never read a book with a lurid title or a magazine with lewd content.

Military corporations impart these instructions to all "repairmen" that are contracted for services in Muslim countries.[3]

Reed knew that if a problem arose there was one last resort for staying alive among the *mujahadeen*. No ceremony is involved in becoming a Muslim. All you need to do is to recite these words in Arabic, *"Ashhadu an la ilaha illa Llah, wa ashhadu anna*

Muhammad rasulu Llah" ("There is no God but Allah, and Muhammad is his prophet"). Once you proclaim these two tenets of the Islamic faith, you are not required to produce further proof of your faith and conviction. This means that neither bin Laden nor any member of his terrorist organization may spill a drop of your blood. It was a resort to which Reed, with no spiritual convictions, was willing to turn.

In July 2003 Reed arrived in the crowded, dirty, fly-infested city of Peshawar in northern Pakistan. His deluxe accommodations at Dean's Hotel were far from luxurious. The room, which bore the sign "For Non-Muslims Only," was small, the mattress stiff, and the air-conditioning out of service. Still, it had a private bath, albeit with scant water pressure, and offered a scenic view of Islamia Road.

The road was lined from dawn to dusk with donkey carts, badly dented Toyotas, bicycles, buses spewing black clouds of diesel fumes, and herds of goats. Before the small shops and stores, bearded merchants peddled prayer mats, *misbahahs* (Islamic "rosaries"), linen shirts, wrapped and unwrapped turbans, carpets, tribal robes and *selhams* (hooded cloaks), *tikkas* (spiced grilled mutton), *naap* (flat bread), goat cheese, fruit (apples, pears, grapes, and pomegranates), *lassi* (a sour milk drink), green and black tea, Russian samovars, ceramic vases, lutes, finger rings from animal horns, circumcision hats, henna paste for skin dying, richly decorated *jambiyyahs* (curved daggers), rifles and handguns, prayer beads, and photographs of Osama bin Laden, "the lion of Islam." The few women who walked through the marketplace wore full burqas in accordance with the imposition of Islamic law (*shariah*) by Muttahida Majilis-i-Amal (MMA), the hard-line alliance of six religious groups that had gained control of the provincial government on October 9, 2002, on a platform of opposition to the US military presence in Pakistan and support for al Qaeda and the Taliban.

Bin Laden's image, Reed discovered, was omnipresent. It appeared in murals on the sides of buildings, on posters nailed to utility pools, and in the windows of stores and shops, along with Urdu slogans such as "Death to Foreign Invaders" and, more ominously, "Allah Commands That We Build the Atom."

The mercenary was warned not to leave his room since the streets were filled with *dacoits*, who viewed all visitors to the city as walking CARE packages, and students from the *madrassahs*, who have taken to heart the teachings of their *muftis* that the killing of all Americans (men, women, and children) has been sanctioned by Allah.[4]

Reed spent the evening before a black-and-white television set with a six-pack of beer, even though alcohol is banned in Pakistan under Islamic law. He had obtained the beer from room service after filling out a form (for non-Muslims only), paying a fee of ten rupees, and waiting in the solitude of his room for the hotel clerk to make the clandestine delivery. He also purchased from the same clerk an ounce of premium Pakistani hash. For this purchase, he was not required to fill out a form or to pay a fee. Hash and heroin are as easy to buy in Peshawar as Milky Way and Snicker candy bars are in Pacoima, California.[5]

At dawn, after the muezzins called the people to morning prayer, armed agents of Kashmir Khan, the most powerful of the tribal leaders and protector of bin Laden,[6] appeared at the door of Reed's room and handed him a traditional *shalwat kameez*—a long, loose-fitting shirt and baggy pants—for the trip to outlying towns and villages of the North-West Frontier Province and a travel permit from the Peshawar Office of Home Security. He darkened his complexion with theatrical greasepaint, changed into the proper clothing, wrapped a white turban about his head, and set off to the great Sulaiman Range along the Indus River in a Toyota pickup truck.

The Pashtuns remain the most dominant tribe in the North-West Frontier Province. They subscribe to the *milmastia*—the Islamic code of hospitality that demands protection for fellow Muslims who seek shelter in their country—even if such shelter means risking their lives.[7] Smugglers, gun runners, drug dealers, thieves, and cutthroats have found safe haven in the province, giving the region a well-deserved reputation for lawlessness. Nearly everyone in the province is armed; even the poorest tribal members carry Kalishnikov rifles. Only a fortunate few—those who can afford *chowkidaars*, or private guards—walk about without a firearm.[8]

On the outskirts of Peshawar, the pickup truck arrived at a checkpoint where a sign in English announced the following: Attention: Entry of Foreigners Is Prohibited beyond This Point. The guards showed the soldiers the requisite authorization; Reed produced his passport and the permit from the Office of Home Security; the gate was opened and the bus was allowed to venture into the "land of the lawless"—a place outside the jurisdiction of all central and provincial governmental agencies.

On the way to Darra Adam Khel, the truck passed hundreds of squalid mud-brick and wattle stalls crowded with bearded and turbaned Pashtun men. Many stalls were brightly painted with the slogan "Long Live Osama!"[9] The sky was thick with a greasy haze of black smoke that came from tire-fed fires, where women in black and purple burqas baked mud bricks. By 9 AM, the temperature reached 105 degrees.

The narrow streets of Darra Adam Khel were lined with ramshackle single-family houses and one-room shops that were decorated with brightly colored pictures of rifles, machine guns, and slogans such as "*Jihad* is an obligation" and "Victory or Martyrdom." Within the shops, gunsmiths worked at forges with foot-powered lathes to produce weapons. The gun barrels were molded from steel manufacturing rods that had been purchased from scrap yards or stolen by bandits from construction sites. Every few minutes the silence was broken by the roar of gunfire as tribesmen tested out new products and cries of *"Allahu akbar"* ("Allah is great").

But Reed was not in search of the heavy Pak imitations of Soviet rifles—imitations that were likely to explode in your face when you pulled the trigger. He wanted high-end goods—goods that had been donated to the Afghan rebels by the CIA or confiscated from the Soviet invaders during the Afghan war—goods such as AK-47s and AK-74s (Soviet assault rifles), Stalin Organ–style RPGs (rocket-propelled grenades) and LAWs (light antitank weapons), and several crates of land mines. Such items were sold in an open marketplace—known as "Smugglers' Bazaar"—on the outskirts of the mountain village.

The marketplace was crowded with men wearing the distinctive black-and-white robes and turbans of the Taliban; the air was pungent with the odors of dung, hashish, grilled meats, diesel fuel, and cordite. Before many tents and stands were pictures of Osama bin Laden, Ayman al-Zawahiri—the "beloved doctor"—Supreme Leader Mullah Mohammed Omar, and "the Magnificent 19"—the terrorists who conducted the 9/11 attack on America.

As soon as Reed emerged from the truck with his two guards, local tribal officials demanded to see his travel permit. Upon discovering that Reed was a new arrival from South Africa, they assumed that he was a CIA agent or *kafir* intruder in search of information about bin Laden. Several tribesmen, in the company of their chieftains, requested the right to kill him instantly. The fatwa against Christians and Jews dictates that there should be no association between the people of the House of Islam (*dar al-Islam*) and the people of the House of War (*dar al-Harb*).[10] Moreover, Osama bin Laden, with his legendary largesse, offered to pay a bounty of thirty thousand dollars for the body of every Christian or Jew, either soldier or civilian.

In their eagerness to serve Allah and collect the award, the tribesmen were placated neither by Reed's insistence that he represented a South African military corporation nor by his guards' recitation of the honored name of Kashmir Khan. Several students from a local *madrassah* expressed their desire to hack off Reed's head for a game of Afghan *buzkashi* (polo).

Reed remembered his instructions. He refrained from making eye contact with the tribesmen and spoke only when addressed in English by the chieftains. Still, the situation continued to worsen. A large group of tribesmen began surrounding him, crying out taunting words in Pashtu, Sindi, and Baluchi, while poking him with their rifles.

Forced to adopt the last resort, Reed uttered the Arabic words that he had committed to memory: *"Ashhadu an la ilaha illa Llah, wa ashhadu anna Muhammad rasulu Llah."* He continued to recite the words with a bowed head. Gradually, the tension dissolved, the crowd dispersed, and the tribal officials welcomed Reed and his guards to the bazaar by offering them *tikkas, naap,* fruit, and *lassi.*

After purchasing several crates of assault rifles, RPGs, LAWs, and land mines at the bus, Reed and his companions loaded the truck and transported the weapons to a warehouse in Islamabad, where, according to Reed, the goods were placed in the care of Pakistani Inter Service Intelligence (ISI) agents.

From Islamabad, they traveled to arms factories and warehouses in Bara and Teerah and places throughout Waziristan, where smiling color photos of bin Laden graced the entranceway of every shop, roadside stand, and dwelling place. In such remote and mountainous places, Reed was presented not only with Soviet weaponry but also newly obtained American goods—M16s, fireproof jackets, night-vision devices, and trekking boots—that had been confiscated from US military headquarters in Afghanistan.

In Bara and Teerah, two villages where people lived in mud

huts without such luxuries as electricity or running water, Afridi chieftains offered state-of-the-art, long-range weapons for sale, including Stinger surface-to-air missiles. One even claimed to have access to a pair of Tomahawk AGM-86Ds, 550 mile-per-hour "smart" bombs—that had been a "present" from the CIA to help the Afghan rebels repel the Soviet invaders. The asking price for the Tomahawks that could be launched from land, air, or sea with a range of 1,553 miles was 96 million rupees ($3 million in US currency).

The offer was mind-boggling. How, Reed wondered, could these backward and illiterate people, living in medieval squalor, possess such sophisticated weaponry? When asked if the offer was legitimate, the chieftain assured Reed that the *mujahadeen* were in possession of even-greater weapons—nuclear weapons—that were being prepared for the next attack on the United States of America.

Such a claim seemed preposterous—almost as preposterous as the turbaned figure in a *shalwat kameez*, attempting to negotiate a multimillion-dollar arms deal before an open campfire in the wilds of the North-West Frontier. The chieftain, according to Reed, went on to say that Russian, Pakistani, and Chinese scientists were training al Qaeda "suicide bombers" in the means of detonating the nuclear suitcases and other nuclear devices. One such training cell, the chieftain said, remains located in an area called Markash, 140 miles north of Gilgit, near the borders of Tajikistan and China.[11]

Reed discovered tidbits of relevant information during his journey, including the present whereabouts of Osama bin Laden. The great warrior, he was assured, remains in the small village of Dir, about fifty miles from the Afghan border on the Kunar Province.[12]

Dir remains within the Malakand Pass, the site of some of the fiercest skirmishes under the British Raj. A Pakistani army fort still stands where the young Winston Churchill shot down rebels and received a citation for heroism. The fort is presently occupied by Maulvi Sufi Mohamed, an old and revered Muslim scholar, who maintains a Taliban-style rule of the area with public executions of adulterers, homosexuals, apostates, and Christian infidels. It is a place where bin Laden and his fellow terrorists feel quite at home.

Bin Laden's latest hiding place remains no secret among the tribesmen. It is proclaimed in the *shabnamas*, or "night letters," that are circulated throughout the North-West Frontier. News of his whereabouts was even published on the front page of the *Daily Ummat*, the leading Urdu language paper of Karachi, on August 10, 2003.[13]

Despite the $25 million bounty that the US government placed on his head—a bounty that is proclaimed by the thousands of Pashtu-language leaflets that are dropped by US aircraft on a daily basis, bin Laden remains not only safe and secure in Dir but free to travel to other parts of the country, including regular trips to Peshawar and several to the smuggler-infested bazaar town of Rebat at the center of "the Devil's Triangle," the conjunction of the borders of Pakistan, Afghanistan, and Iran.[14] No Muslim will dare to capture or kill him—not even a squadron of elite military personnel from the Musharraf government, let alone a group of professional bounty hunters. It is the duty of all Muslims to honor the revered leader of the *mujahadeen* and the $25 million reward comes with the price tag of apostasy and eternal damnation.[15] Even when Pakistani soldiers and ISI officials receive confirmation of the location of top-level Taliban and al Qaeda operatives, they display no inclination to make arrests—not even when such figures appear in the streets of Peshawar.[16]

What's more, any concerted attempt by the United States to invade any part of the North-West Frontier Province by crossing the 680-mile border between Afghanistan and Pakistan in an effort to capture bin Laden will be met by the resistance of the vast majority of the twenty million Muslims who inhabit the formidable area. A Taliban operative by the name of Zabihullah assured *Newsweek* reporters that bin Laden will never be arrested and dragged before the press in the manner of Saddam Hussein: "We have a strongly Islamic population, thousands of high mountains, and millions of caves to hide in. Wherever bin Laden stops, he tells his followers to plant land mines and pockets of high explosives. These booby traps are meant to protect him and also to make sure that the sheik cannot escape; that he will be quickly martyred; and that he will never be captured alive."[17]

Reed, in any case, was not about to seek the reward. The way to Dir remains strewn with the bodies of several would-be bounty hunters. They have been cast in the pines beside the dirt road. All have been tortured, stripped naked, and castrated. Their eyeballs have been plucked from their sockets; their ears have been hacked off; and their tongues have been ripped from their mouths. Notes have been taped to the groin of every victim. "Do not be angry or shocked," the notes say in Pashtu. "These are the bodies of agents of the USA."

CHAPTER 7

THE UNION OF RADICAL ISLAM

I believe that our North-West Frontier Province presents, at this moment, a spectacle unique in the world; at least I know of no other spot where after twenty-five years of peaceful occupation, a great civilized power has obtained so little influence over its semi-savage neighbors, and acquired so little knowledge of them, that the country within a day's ride of its important garrison is an absolute terra incognita and that there is absolutely no security for British life a mile or two beyond our border.

—Lord Lytton, April 22, 1877

The Taliban used to be wary of Osama bin Laden and his brand of hard-line internationalized militancy. Their project was limited to Afghanistan and they bore no ill-feeling to America or the West. Now they see themselves as a key element in the supposed struggle against an aggressive "Zionist-Christian Alliance."
"Bin Laden is the greatest mujahid *[holy warrior] and all Muslims think he is their ideal," said Mullah Abdul Rauf, the Taliban official. "All those fighting a* jihad *anywhere in the world against the cruel infidels are our brothers and allies."*

—James Burke, *Observer*, November 16, 2003

As soon as the United States launched Operation Enduring Freedom on October 7, 2001, something monumental began to take place throughout the North-West Frontier Province. For centuries, this remained the land of *badal*, where every Mohmandi Pashtun, Shiniwari, Achakzai, Yusufzai, and Khyber Afridi was obliged to avenge a wrong no matter how slight or how it long it would take. Every major tribal home represented a small mud-and-stone fortress where family members stood watch day and night in a tower. Pashtu is the only known language in which the word for "cousin" is the same as the word for "enemy."[1] An American journalist, traveling through tribal territories in 1999, recounted an incident concerning a Pashtu woman who was seen kissing her Shiniwar cousin on a hillside. The father of the girl, upon hearing of this incident, captured the couple, tied them both to a tree, and pumped seventy-five bullets into them.[2]

But with the appearance of the US invaders in Afghanistan, the tribesmen began setting aside their differences to join together in the great *jihad* of the bin Laden Brotherhood. This unification was evidenced by the million-man marches in support of al Qaeda and the Taliban that took place in Lahore and the capital cities of Pakistan throughout 2003; by the stunning victories of the Muttahida Majilis-I-Amal (MMA)—an alliance of six Islamic religious groups—in recent elections;[3] and by the thousands of stands and stalls throughout the countryside where Pashtuns stand side by side with Shiniwaris to raise money for the Taliban's reconquest of Afghanistan.

A significant development in the unification of radical Islam for al Qaeda's great *jihad*, as noted earlier, came with the alliance of Gulbuddin Hekmatyar, the richest and most powerful of the Pashtun warlords, with bin Laden and Mullah Omar (see chapter 1). During the Afghan war against the Soviet Union, Hekmatyar and his tribe of Muslim extremists—the Hezb-e-Islami—received more than $600 million from the United States and an equal sum from the Saudi government to aid the guerrilla resistance.[4] As a goodwill offering, the United States also provided Hekmatyar with hundreds of Stinger missiles. The missiles proved to be the most effective weapon in the struggle against the Soviets. They represented easy-to-use, "fire and forget" weapons that locked onto the heat radiated by helicopters and airplane engines. When the Afghans began to deploy the Stingers in 1986, the Soviets lost their air superiority and the tide of the war turned against them. Graham Fuller, the CIA bureau chief in Kabul, later recalled: "The decision to give Stingers was controversial. It marked an escalation of the confrontation with the Soviets. John McMahon, the deputy director [of the CIA] was opposed to doing it. For him, geopolitical concerns were the most important. The Soviet war could be taken into Pakistan. He was less concerned about the technology giveaway."[5]

After the war, Hekmatyar became prime minister of Afghanistan under President Burhanuddin Rabbani. With his newly acquired power and prominence, the warlord reestablished the drug routes to Turkey, Iran, and Chechnya and became one of the wealthiest figures in the Muslim world.

In 1994, Hekmatyar initiated a coup against the Rabbani government that resulted in a yearlong siege of Kabul. During the first two months of the siege, four thousand residents of Kabul were killed, twenty-one thousand injured, and two hundred thousand were forced to flee the capital city with their belongings. Mullah Omar and the Taliban came to the rescue of the besieged city by trashing Hekmatyar's army in 1995 and forcing the warlord to seek shelter in Iran.

The vanquished and exiled Hekmatyar turned for help to his old friends at the CIA in his effort to mount a campaign to oust Mullah Omar and his brigade of ragged and rabid student militants from

Afghanistan—even pledging his willingness to restore Rabbani's government. But US intelligence officials turned a deaf ear to such requests, believing that the interests of the United States were better served by the one-eyed mullah than by the troublesome warlord.

The shunning of Hekmatyar became even more apparent when he failed to receive an invitation to an international conference in Bonn, where US officials intended to address Pashtun concerns regarding the transitional government in Afghanistan. From Iran, Hekmatyar fumed that "only groups fitting to US requirements and interests have been invited to Bonn."[6] On January 8, 2003, he responded to the slight by issuing his own call for *jihad* against the American invaders:

> The Afghan *mujahadeen* have made a pledge with their God that they will force the Americans out of Afghanistan in the same way as they forced the Russians out. They have vowed not to lay down their arms and let their enemies rest for a single moment until they liberate the country and oust the invading force from every inch of the country. . . .
>
> We should once again make it clear to all the Afghans that as long as the Americans are governing our country and foreign forces dominate our country, we have no intention of fighting the interim administration or any other Afghan group, even those who have committed great national treachery and historic crimes. We do not want to waste our time and resources by engaging them in futile clashes. At the moment, we only stress the need for incessant and indefatigable *jihad* against the invading forces and invite everyone to this *jihad*.[7]

Shortly after issuing the fatwa, Hekmatyar met with bin Laden, al-Zawahiri, and Mullah Omar in the village of Shah Salim, about thirty miles west of the Pakistani city of Chitral, near the border of Afghanistan's Kunar Province, to form a new alliance among al

Qaeda, the Taliban, and Hezb-e-Islami that would be called Fateh Islam ("Islamic Victory").[8] The first step in the battle plan called for the regaining of control of the drug routes with the compliance of corrupt border guards.[9] Bin Laden had set about to accomplish this task almost as soon as he established a new base of operations in Pakistan in 2002. The second step of Fateh Islam consisted of a series of guerilla attacks in eastern Afghanistan—attacks that culminated in a battle near Spin Boldak on January 27, 2003.[10]

The new alliance proved to be an incredible boon for bin Laden. Hekmatyar brought to the *jihad* not only weapons and an army but also the great wealth that he had amassed, in part, from American taxpayers through the largesse of the CIA. "Hekmatyar has more money than anyone," Haji Abdul Zahukl, a *mujahadeen* commander told the *Boston Globe*, "and he thought about the future. He invested in business [primarily the drug trade] and he saved it."[11]

The most pressing need of al Qaeda, according to intelligence sources, remains cash, despite the fact that millions continue to flow into coffers of the *mujahadeen* from the opium fields, the Saudi Arabians, and the funneling of Muslim charities throughout the world. The great attack of 9/11 was an enormous strategic and financial success. It resulted in the death of 2,292 Americans, urban devastation in excess of $16.5 billion in public and private funds, and the loss of two hundred thousand jobs.[12] The long-range results were even more significant. By 2003, the war on terror was costing the American public $4.5 billion a month,[13] and the national debt rose to $6.8 trillion.[14] Moreover, the travel industry was cut to the quick, with airline companies hemorrhaging more than $13 billion annually.[15] All of this was accomplished by al Qaeda for a mere pittance—less than $500,000. Assessing the operation, bin Laden said:

> I say the events that happened on Tuesday, September 11, in New York and Washington, that is truly a great event in all measures, and its claims until this moment are not over and are still contin-

111

uing. . . . According to their own admissions, the share of the losses on the Wall Street market reached 16 percent. They said that this number is a record, which has never happened since the opening of the market more than 230 years ago. This large collapse has never happened. The gross amount that is traded in that market reaches $4 trillion. So if we multiply 16 percent by $4 trillion to find out the loss that affected the stocks, it reaches $640 billion of losses from stocks, by Allah's grace. So this amount, for example, is the budget of the Sudan for 640 years. They have lost this, due to an attack that happened with the success of Allah lasting one hour only.[16]

The 9/11 terrorists kept costs at a minimum—staying at forty-dollar-a-night motels and eating at Denny's. Their only extravagances were the tens of thousands spent on flying lessons and passenger-jet flight simulation.[17]

Terrorism, by definition, is "asymmetrical warfare" that rarely requires huge sums of money. The estimated cost of the bomb that exploded beneath the World Trade Center in 1993, killing six and causing half a billion in damages, was less than $3,000.[18] In 1998, when an al Qaeda operative was sent from Pakistan to foment terrorist attacks within the United States, he was allotted a total of $12,000 for travel and expenses.[19]

But in preparing for the next attack on US soil, bin Laden has been obliged to provide a king's ransom in costs. He has paid an amount estimated from $60 to $100 million to obtain the expertise of Pakistan's nuclear engineers and the collaboration of generals and members of the Pakistani secret service (ISI), and a similar amount for the services of former Soviet and Chinese nuclear scientists and technicians.[20] Combined with these expenses have been the tremendous costs of setting up infrastructures for the construction of nuclear bombs and other weapons of mass destruction, and the exorbitant cost of buying fissionable uranium and plutonium from black market sources. One purchase of twelve kilos of uranium-235 from a Ukrainian arms dealer reportedly cost bin Laden more than $75 million.[21]

Al Qaeda's present need of funds has been heightened by the fact that Russian traffickers posing as atomic engineers managed to bilk bin Laden out of over $200 million. The traffickers sold representatives of al Qaeda uranium that was not usable for a nuclear weapon and a nuclear by-product that they presented as "Red Mercury," a supposedly essential ingredient for a secret weapon. Bin Laden was not the only dupe in the scam. The same Russian traffickers managed to sell stocks of the mysterious Red Mercury at extravagant prices to representatives of Iraqi interests.[22]

Bin Laden, of course, is not interested in the processing and production of fissile material from radioactive substances. Such an undertaking would require a massive technological infrastructure and the required resources of an industrialized nation. Even al Qaeda, with its millions from the drug trade, could not undertake such an operation. Bin Laden is rather seeking to avoid the difficulties of producing fissile material to build nuclear weapons by purchasing nuclear weapons that already have been built.

Most nuclear states exercise strict security control over their nuclear arsenals. These controls include electronic safeguards that are built into the weapons to make an unauthorized detonation impossible. Bin Laden has managed to obtain such weapons in the form of nuclear suitcase bombs from the Chechen Mafia. Still, he requires the expertise of former SPETSNAZ (Soviet special forces) personnel and nuclear technicians from Russia, North Korea, China, and Pakistan to upgrade and replenish the nuclear cores of the weapons and to devise means of detonation for al Qaeda operatives, including the wiring of suicide bombers as one method.

With the fissile materials that bin Laden purchased and continues to purchase from black market sources, al Qaeda remains actively engaged in producing atomic bombs that have explosive yields in excess of ten kilotons. Viable designs for such weapons have been available from public domain sources for many years. In 1967 the CIA conducted an experiment to see if three newly graduated physics students, equipped with forty pounds of highly enriched uranium, could build a viable fission weapon from information available at local libraries. The three students managed to complete the task successfully in a makeshift laboratory in less than thirty months.[23] With the sophisticated designs presently available from the Internet, Dr. Graham Allison, director of the Belfer Center for Science and International Affairs at Harvard University, maintains that similar students could produce a similar nuclear device in a matter of months.[24]

In addition to the above, bin Laden has devoted considerable time and expense to the creation of radiological weapons. In videotapes secured from an al Qaeda safe house in Kabul, large canisters are displayed with markings indicating that they contain radioactive material.[25] Radiological weapons utilize conventional explosives to disperse radioactive material and are "almost childishly simple" to construct.[26] They are capable of producing neither nuclear chain reactions nor other associated large releases of energy. For this reason, the detonation of such a devise would not result in the killing of hundreds of thousands of people. Still, such bombs are capable of spreading radioactive contamination over vast portions of metropolitan areas, causing "a panicky evacuation, a gradual increase in cancer rates, a staggeringly expensive cleanup, [and] possibly the need to demolish whole neighborhoods."[27]

In 2002, as the great coming together of the *mujahadeen* began to take place, the world witnessed a sharp increase in al Qaeda terrorism as evidenced by the following events:

February 14: Afghanistan's air transport and tourism minister Abdul Rahman was beaten to death at the Kabul Airport in an assassination sanctioned by bin Laden and Mullah Omar.[28]

March 17: The Protestant International Church in Islamabad was bombed, killing five, including the wife and daughter of US diplomat Milton Green. Forty more were wounded.[29] The attack coincided with the visit of Gen. Tommy Franks to Pakistan.

April 8: Afghanistan's defense minister Mohammad Fahim survived a bomb assassination attempt in Jalalabad. Four others were killed.

April 11: A truck exploded near El Ghriba synagogue on the southern Tunisian island of Djerba, killing fourteen Germans, five Tunisians, and a Frenchman. In an audiotape message, Sulaiman Abu Ghaith, a spokesman for al Qaeda, boasted that the American invasion of Afghanistan was the cause of the bombing. "Our martyrs are ready for operations against American and Jewish targets inside and outside," Abu Gharth said. "America should be prepared. It should be ready. They [the Americans] should fasten their seat belts. We are coming to them where they never expected. The current American administration every once in a while releases terrorist attack warnings. I say yes, yes, to what the American officials are saying that we are going to launch attacks against Americans." The al Qaeda spokesman went on to offer his assurance that bin Laden and al-Zawahiri remained "in good health" and were not injured at Tora Bora.[30]

May 8: A bus bombing outside the Sheraton Hotel in Karachi killed fourteen, including French nationals, and injured forty-five, including a US Marine. In a handwritten statement delivered to the press in Karachi, a group calling itself al-Qanoon—Arabic for "the Law"—claimed responsibility for the bombing. al-Qanoon proved to be most likely an alias for al Qaeda.[31]

June 14: A car bomb outside the US consulate in Karachi killed fourteen and injured fifty-one more. The explosion came on the heels of a visit by US defense secretary Donald Rumsfeld, who left the region on June 12 after visiting Indian and Pakistani officials to ease tensions between the nuclear-armed rivals. Pakistani police blamed the International Movement of the Mujahadeen, an ally of al Qaeda.[32]

July 6: Abdul Qadir, one of the three Afghan vice presidents, was shot dead in Kabul. Ten guards, appointed by Qadir's predecessors at the Public Works Ministry, were arrested.[33]

September 5: An explosion in Kabul killed 32 and injured 150 more. An hour later, Afghan president Hamid Karzai survived an assassination attempt in Kandahar where he was attending a wedding celebration for his youngest brother. American troops killed the gunman. Investigators traced both bombings to Gulbuddin Hekmatyar and the Hezb-e-Islami.[34]

October 2: Four people, including an American Green Beret commando, were killed and twenty-four injured in an open-air karaoke bar in Zamboanga on Mindanao Island in the Philippines. The attack was assumed to be made in reaction to the 260 US troops who were deployed to the area to improve the Philippine army's ability to fight terrorist organizations. Abu Sayyaf, a terrorist group in league with al Qaeda, claimed responsibility for the bombing.[35]

October 6: An explosives-laden barge rammed into the French oil tanker *Limburg* off the coast of al-Mukalla in Yemen. One Bulgarian crew member died, and ninety thousand barrels of oil were spilled into the Gulf of Aden.[36]

October 8: Two al Qaeda terrorists attacked US Marines at an island training facility in Kuwait. One Marine was killed.[37] The incident served as an indicator that the *mujahadeen* intended to offer its assistance to ward off the US invasion of Iraq.

October 10: Terror returned to Zamboanga in the Philippines

when a bomb exploded in a crowded bus station. Six were killed and ten wounded. Blame again was attributed to Abu Sayyaf.[38]

October 12: A year almost to the day after President Bush launched Operation Enduring Freedom, bombs exploded outside two nightclubs in Kuna Beach, Bali, killing 202 and wounding hundreds more. One hundred of the dead were Australians. A third bomb exploded near the US consulate in Sanur, several miles from Kuna Beach, without causing casualties. Jemaah Islamiyah, a banned Islamic group with ties to al Qaeda, claimed responsibility.[39]

October 16: Five small package bombs exploded at government offices in Karachi. A sixth went off at a police station. Nine Pakistanis were wounded.[40]

October 17: Zamboanga got hit for the third time in two weeks by Abu Sayyaf terrorists, when a bomb exploded in a department store, killing 6 and injuring 144.[41]

October 18: A bomb exploded in Manila, killing two and wounding twenty. Commenting on the incident, CIA director George Tenet said: "When you see multiple attacks that you have seen occur around the world from Bali to Kuwait, the number of failed attacks that have been attempted, and the various messages that have been issued by senior al Qaeda leaders, you must make the assumption that al Qaeda is in an execution phase and intends to strike us here and overseas."[42]

November 28: Fifteen were killed in a car bomb attack on a hotel frequented by Israeli tourists in the Kenyan port city of Mombasa. Two of the suicide bombers were identified as Abdullah Ahmed Abdullah and Faed Ali Sayam, who appeared on the FBI's list of most wanted al Qaeda terrorists.[43] Shortly after the bomb exploded, two surface-to-air Strela missiles were fired at a chartered Israeli airliner that had been taking tourists back to Israel. The missiles barely missed their target.

In 2003, manifestations of al Qaeda terrorism became more widespread, even extending to "apostles"—Muslim extremists inside and outside the Middle East. Commenting on this development, Steven Simon, a counterterrorism expert with the US National Security Council, said: "The movement has metastasized well beyond the organizational boundaries of al Qaeda. Innumerable local groups now subscribe to the bin Laden agenda. The group has done its work. It has spurred a worldwide insurgency."[44] The following is a listing of the most significant events:

January 6, 2003: UK terror police discovered a large amount of ricin—a poison that in small amounts is twice as potent as cobra venom—in a London apartment. The discovery led to two raids: the first on a London mosque; the second on an apartment occupied by six North African Muslims in Manchester. During the course of the second raid, a police officer was shot and killed. The incident, according to Russian defense minister Sergei Ivanov, proved that al Qaeda's attempts to obtain weapons of mass destruction represented a "real threat."[45]

January 21: Terrorists planted bombs that destroyed two massive gas pipelines in Sui, Pakistan. A huge crater—sixty feet in diameter and twenty-five feet deep—provided proof of the massive amount of cordite explosives that were placed under the pipes. "There is no doubt that terrorists with high expertise in handing explosives have been hired by local warlords to destroy the Sui gas pipeline," said former Pakistani air marshal Ayaz Ahmed Khan.[46]

January 21: An American civilian was killed and another critically wounded in a highway ambush near the US military complex in Kuwait.[47]

February 22: Three al Qaeda terrorists opened fire on a group of Shiites watching a World Cup cricket match outside an *imambaragh* (Shiite house of worship) in Karachi, Pakistan. Nine were killed.[48]

February 28: A gunman fired on Pakistani police guarding the US consulate in Karachi, killing three officers and wounding six, including a bystander.[49]

March 4: A bomb exploded at Davao Airport in the Philippines, killing sixteen and wounding fifty-two. Among the dead were three US civilians, including a Christian missionary. Davao was believed to be safe from terror attacks because of Mayor Rodrigo Duterte's close association with Islamic extremist groups. Several months before the incident, Duterte told members of Abu Sayyaf—a group in league with al Qaeda—that they were welcome to the city for rest and recreation but advised them not to "do your shit here."[50] The terrorists ignored his advice.

April 3: Another bomb exploded in Davao—this one killing sixteen and wounding fifty-two. Blame was placed on the Moro Islamic Liberation Front.[51]

May 10: A suicide bomber killed thirteen and injured forty in Koronadal on Mindanao Island. Abu Sayyaf claimed responsibility. Mindanao Island is home to eight million Philippine Muslims. It is one of the poorest regions of the Philippines.[52]

May 12: Thirty-four people were killed and two hundred injured by a series of bomb attacks in Saudi Arabia's capital, Riyadh. The attacks were aimed at luxury compounds that house foreign nationals. The blasts coincided with a visit to the kingdom by US secretary of state Colin Powell. Ali Abdul Rahman al-Faqaasi, a member of al Qaeda's inner circle, was placed under arrest. The death toll would have been considerably higher but many residents of the complex—all the employees of a US military contractor—were out on an exercise with the Saudi military. Among those arrested was Ali Abdul Rahman al-Ghamdi, a top al Qaeda operative, who served with bin Laden at Tora Bora.[53]

May 16: A dozen suicide bombers, using crude homemade explosives stuffed into backpacks, blew themselves up at five locations in Casablanca, killing 41 and wounding 201.[54] One location was a Spanish restaurant; another was a Jewish social club. Abdel Moulsbbat, the suspected mastermind behind the bombings, died in police custody.

June 7: Four German peacekeepers were killed and sixty wounded by a suicide attack on a bus in Kabul. The attack was the deadliest assault on International Security Assistance Forces since they arrived in Afghanistan to bolster the government of President Hamid Karzai.[55]

July 4: Three gunmen massacred fifty-three members of the Hazara tribe in an *imambaragh* at Quetta, the capital of the Baluchistan Province of Pakistan. It came on the heels of the murder of eleven Hazaras undergoing police training in the same city. The massacre represented yet another attempt by al Qaeda and the Taliban to drive out the Hazaras from the province since members of this Shiite tribe had been a major source of information about bin Laden's activities in the North-West Frontier Province and Baluchistan.[56]

July 18: Eight Afghan government soldiers were killed during a surprise Taliban attack in the southeastern Khost Province.[57]

July 30: Taliban gunmen killed Mawlavi Jenab, a member of the Ulema Shura (clerics' council), outside a mosque in Kandahar. Gen. Mohammad Salim, Kandahar's security chief, admitted that the assassination represented the third bloody attack on members of the council since it announced early in 2003 that the Afghanistan *jihad* was over and that Muslims should support the US-backed government that replaced the Taliban.[58]

August 5: Ten people were killed and seventy-four injured when a bomb exploded at the luxurious J. W. Marriott Hotel in the Indonesian capital of Jakarta. Defense Minister Matori Abdul Djalil blamed the militant group Jemaah Islamiyah, an organization with strong ties to al Qaeda.[59]

August 7: Taliban soldiers executed six Afghan soldiers and a driver for the US-based aid agency Mercy Corps in Helmand.[60]

August 13: Helmand was also the site of the next terrorist attack when a bomb blew apart a bus, killing fifteen, including six children.[61]

August 18: Just hours after a deadly raid on a police station killed twenty-two in a province south of Kabul, al Qaeda and Taliban fighters mounted an attack on another police compound, setting it ablaze and taking four policemen hostage.[62]

October 1: The Taliban threatened to cut off the noses and ears of men who shave their beards and anyone caught listening to music. Groups of Taliban operatives began stopping vehicles and visiting villagers throughout southeastern Afghanistan and the North-West Frontier Province to make sure that the people were obeying the orders.[63]

October 3: A Taliban operative attacked a group of Shiite Muslims in Karachi, Pakistan. Six were killed. The incident represented further retaliation by the Taliban against the Shiites, who were collecting information for US intelligence agencies.[64]

November 8: Al Qaeda again turned its attention to Riyadh as another upscale housing complex was bombed. Twenty-eight people, including five children, were killed, and over one hundred injured. In a statement e-mailed to the London-based Arab newspaper *Al-Quds al-Arabi*, bin Laden said: "The Riyadh compound was inhabited by Arab translators working for American intelligence. We have warned Muslims more than once that they must not go near the places where the infidels are found, and we renew that warning. It is not permitted to mix with these infidels until they have put a halt to their Crusade."[65]

November 15: Two car bombs exploded outside synagogues in central Istanbul, killing twenty-nine. An Arabic newspaper said the Brigades of the Martyr Abu Hafz al-Masri claimed responsibility.[66]

November 21: Abu Hafz al-Masri struck again by bombing the

London-based HSBC bank and the British consulate in Istanbul, killing thirty-two and injuring four hundred.[67] Fevzi Yitiz, a key suspect in the bombings, told Turkish police that some of the conspirators met with bin Laden before the attacks and that the al Qaeda leader urged them to attack the Incirlik Air Base in southern Turkey that was used by the United States for the invasion of Iraq. Yitiz said that the attackers dropped their plans to bomb Incirlik due to the high degree of security that was in place at the air base and opted, instead, to focus on the civilian targets.[68]

December 4: Al Qaeda tried to destabilize the Saudi government by a series of assassination attempts against top security officials. One victim, Maj. Gen. Abdelaziz al-Huweirini, was shot and seriously injured on December 4.[69]

December 6: A bomb exploded at a bazaar in Kandahar, wounding twenty and demolishing six shops. To curb the new onslaught of attacks, US forces launched an air raid over the village of Atola in the eastern Ghazni Province of Afghanistan. The air raid resulted in the deaths of nine children and a suspected Taliban fighter. Four days later, the United States conducted a second air raid—this time in the eastern province of Paktia. The raid resulted in the killing of six children and two adults.[70]

December 14: An attempt to assassinate Pakistani president Musharraf came within a whisper of success. The BBC called the incident a "reminder of the vulnerability of some of Washington's key allies."[71]

December 25: President Musharraf narrowly escaped death again when al Qaeda operatives rammed into his motorcade with two cars filled with explosives. The incident took place at a gas station in Islamabad. Fourteen people were killed and forty-six injured. The latest assassination attempts appeared to stem from al-Zawahiri's audiotaped message in which he called upon "all believers" to rid the world of "the apostate Musharraf." This message was broadcast on radio stations throughout the Arab world.[72] Since coming to power in October 1999, Musharraf had been the target of eight assassination attempts. The common opinion among journalists today is that his luck is running out.[73]

Throughout the winter and early spring of 2004, al Qaeda began to amass a vast Euro army. In France the terrorist group managed to attract between thirty-five thousand and forty-five thousand new recruits who were organized into military-style units. The units met regularly at scattered locations for training in the use of weapons, explosives, and chemical/biological warfare.[74] In Germany, al Qaeda gained thirty thousand new recruits; in Great Britain, ten thousand.[75] Bin Laden's agents have been less active in Italy because the terrorist organization maintains a thriving presence next door in the Balkans, where arms, equipment, money, and false documentation are easily secreted to European cells.[76] The number of new recruits in Belgium, Switzerland, Holland, Sweden, and Norway remains unknown.

On March 11, 2004, the most brutal terrorist attack since 9/11 occurred in Madrid, where bombs were set off in three crowded commuter trains, killing 201 and injuring 1,400. The attack caused a public uproar that resulted in the resounding defeat of Spain's prime minister Jose Maria Aznar and his Popular Party in the March 14 election. Aznar had been a staunch supporter of President Bush and the invasion of Iraq.[77] The Brigade of the Martyr Abu Hafz al-Masri, a branch of al Qaeda that is directly controlled by bin Laden,[78] assumed responsibility for the attack and issued the following statement to the Arabic newspaper *Al-Quds al-Arabi*:

> This is part of settling old accounts within Spain, the crusader, and America's ally in its war against Islam. Aznar, where is America? Who will protect you, Britain, Japan, Italy and others from us?

When we attacked the Italian troops in Nasiriyah and sent you and America's agents an ultimatum to withdraw from the anti-Islam alliance, you did not understand the message. Now we have made it clear and hope that this time you will understand.

We, at the Abu Hafz brigades, have not felt sad for the so-called civilians. Is it OK for you to kill our children, women, old people, and youth in Afghanistan, Iraq, Palestine, and Kashmir. And is it forbidden to us to kill yours?

We announce the good news for Muslims in the world that the strike of the black wind of death, the expected strike against America, is now at its final stage—90 percent ready—and it is coming soon.[79]

The attack in Madrid remained in keeping with the statements contained in the stream of fatwas that spewed forth from al Qaeda since December 2002, three months before the invasion of Iraq. Spain was singled out as the second European target on the list—the first target being Turkey.[80] Turkey gained predominance over all other operating theaters since bin Laden and his fellow Islamic fanatics felt constrained to recover the honor and glory of the Ottoman caliphates that were trampled by Western forces in 1917 during the closing days of World War I. Two terrorist outbreaks that killed 63 and injured 600 more took place in Istanbul in November 2003. On March 10, 2004, the day of the attacks in Madrid, al Qaeda continued its attacks in Turkey by dispatching two suicide bombers to a building in the Asian section of the city that housed a Masonic lodge. The bombers intended to enter a conference chamber and to detonate the explosives during a lodge meeting. The meeting, however, had been postponed at the last minute, causing the bombers to blow themselves up at the door of an empty restaurant, killing a waiter.[81]

Spain remained the second European target because a goal of al Qaeda is the recovery of the lost Muslim kingdom of "Andalusia." At the start of the great crusades in 1096, three-quarters of Spain was Muslim. Three hundred years later, Ferdinand and Isabella completed the Christian conquest of Spain and ordered the expulsion of all Muslims from the country. This humiliation has never been forgotten in the Arab world.[82]

After Spain, according to the fatwas, the next target in Europe will be Rome, the world center of heresy because of the Vatican and the pope.[83] And the fourth European target will be Vienna because the advancing Muslim armies were defeated there in 1643 before they could engulf the heart of Europe.[84]

While the liberation of lands once held by Muslim rulers remains a goal of al Qaeda, the religious edicts mandate that the *mujahadeen* must never lose sight of its primary objectives: the destruction of Israel, doubly anathematized as a Jewish state in a country once governed by Muslims, and the great Satan, the United States of America, that perpetuates the suppression of Islamic peoples throughout the world.[85]

While bin Laden remains within the North-West Frontier Province, other al Qaeda operatives have sought shelter in Iran, which shares a six-hundred-mile border with Afghanistan. Al Qaeda represents the Sunni faction of Islam; Iran remains predominantly Shiite. These two factions have been at odds since the appointment of Ali, Muhammad's son-in-law, as the fourth caliph in 656 CE. The intensity of the animosity between the groups was crystallized when Shiites united with the Christian infidels to fight the Sunni army of Nur ed-Din during the second crusade.[86]

But in recent years Shiites and Sunnis have begun to set aside their differences in order to unite under Osama bin Laden and his *jihad* against the United States. This development, as counterterrorism experts Daniel Benjamin and Steven Simon point out in *The Age of Sacred Terror*, is extraordinary.[87]

To be sure, the two groups have united several times in the past, most notably, under the banner of the great Saladin ("the rectifier of the faith") during the course of the third crusade and, more recently, with the union of the Palestinian Islamic Jihad and the Iranian Hezbollah in attacks on Israelis. But the majority of fundamentalist Sunnis continue to view their Shiite counterparts as heretics who must be put to death.[88] This was evidenced by the slaughter of fifty-three Shiites by Taliban warriors in Quetta, the capital of the Baluchistan Province of Pakistan, on July 4, 2003.[89]

In 1994, bin Laden began to seek the support of radical Shiite groups in Iran by meeting with Imad Mughniya, Hezbollah's chief terrorist, in Sudan.[90] As noted earlier, a pledge of cooperation was made between the two premier terrorists, and subsequent meetings led to a financial agreement regarding the flow of drugs from Afghanistan to Turkey through the northern region of Iran. The union of al Qaeda with Hezbollah was further strengthened by the US invasions of Afghanistan and Iraq and by the opposition of Shiite clerics to the pro-Western policies of Iranian president Mohammad Khatami, who shocked the Iranian ayatollahs by his appointment of a woman as vice president when he assumed office in 1997.[91]

In the wake of the US assault on Tora Bora in December 2001, Saad bin Laden, Osama's eldest son; Yaaz bin Sifat, a top-ranking al Qaeda planner; Mohammed Islam Haani, the mayor of Kabul during the Taliban regime; Saif al-Adel, the military commander of al Qaeda; Abu Musab al-Zarqawi, the al Qaeda operative in charge of attacks on Europe, along with five hundred al Qaeda and Taliban soldiers, scaled the mountains in the south along the Afghanistan-Pakistan border, then cut through Afghanistan's southernmost provinces to head west toward the border with Iran, where they found safe haven.[92] Al-Zawahiri, bin Laden's top lieutenant, was also spotted in Iran, where he reportedly donned the disguise of an Iranian cleric with a black turban and a dyed beard.[93]

To facilitate the escape from Pakistan, two officials from Pakistan's Passport Agency provided al Qaeda and Taliban operatives with hundreds of false passports. After the arrest of the officials, President Musharraf called the passport incident "very disturbing" and pledged to implement sophisticated measures to prevent future forgeries.[94]

Within Iran, the al Qaeda terrorists were able not only to move about quite freely but also to orchestrate continuous waves of terrorist attacks. On November 8, 2003, Saif al-Qaif initiated the bombing of the residential compound in Riyadh via satellite phone from a village in northern Iran.[95]

President Khatami and other members of the Iranian government, after months of denials, admitted in May 2003 that numerous al Qaeda and Taliban operatives had crossed into their country and that the operatives had been placed "in custody." This reluctant admission prompted a White House official to say: "We know that al Qaeda individuals are inside Iran. But what is the definition of custody? If they are in Iran, free to plan and direct attacks, such as the Saudi bombing, and are able to receive information and updates, that is not custody. That is safe haven."[96] Similarly, US defense secretary Donald Rumsfeld said: "There is no question there have been and are today senior al Qaeda leaders in Iran. And they're busy!"[97]

The al Qaeda guests remain in safe houses controlled by SAVAMA, the Iranian intelligence services.[98] These villas in southern Iran, with saunas and swimming pools, are lavish even by American standards. But despite continuous pressure from the United States, President Khatami lacks the power to dislodge the "guests" from their comfortable new quarters, let alone the muscle to deport them to Saudi Arabia. Khatami, whose term of office will end in 2005, is not seeking reelection. National security officials maintain that he is a "lame duck" and that the mullahs remain in control of the government.[99]

But the most important development in the coming together of radical Islam was neither the union of tribesmen throughout Pakistan and Afghanistan nor the setting aside of the major differences between Sunnis and Shiites. It was rather mentioned by another news item that, by and large, escaped the attention of the international press, namely, the alliance of Osama bin Laden with Dr. Abdul Qadeer Khan, Pakistan's most revered nuclear scientist and, in the opinion of some intelligence experts, "the most dangerous man in the world."[100]

CHAPTER 8

DR. STRANGELOVE

*The plan is going ahead, and, God willing, it is being imple-
mented. But it is a huge task, which is beyond the will and comprehension of human beings. If God's help is with us, this will
happen within a short period of time; keep in mind this prediction. This is not a matter of weapons. We are hopeful for God's
help. The real matter is the extinction of America. And, God
willing, it [America] will fall to the ground.*
    —Mullah Mohammed Omar, November 14, 2001

*O Muslims, take matters firmly against the embassies of America,
England, Australia, and Norway and their interests, companies,
and employees. Burn the ground under their feet, as they should
not enjoy your protection, safety, or security. Expel those criminals out of your countries. Do not allow the Americans, the
British, the Australians, the Norwegians, and the other crusaders
who killed your brothers in Iraq to live in your countries, enjoy
their resources, and wreak havoc in them. Learn from your nineteen brothers who attacked America in its planes in New York and
Washington and caused it a tribulation that it never witnessed
before and is still suffering from its injuries until today. O Iraqi
people, we defeated those crusaders several times before and
expelled them out of our countries and holy shrines. You should*

know that you are not alone in this battle. Your mujahid *brothers are tracking your enemies and lying in wait for them. The* mujahadeen *in Palestine, Afghanistan, and Chechnya and even in the heart of America and the West are causing death to those crusaders. The coming days will bring to you the news that will heal your breasts, God willing.*

—Ayman al-Zawahiri, May 21, 2003

In 1998, Pakistan officially joined the elite nuclear club of nations along with the United States, Russia, China, Great Britain, France, India, and Israel by the successful testing of five atomic bombs beneath the scorched hills of the Baluchistan desert. Military experts throughout the world were shocked to the quick by this demonstration of technology from a third world country that had failed to develop an adequate sanitation system for its major cities. The remarkable technological achievement was accomplished largely through the efforts of one individual, Dr. Abdul Qadeer Khan, a Pakistani scientist and an Islamic extremist.

Dr. Khan, who went on to work on the successful test firings of the nuclear-capable Ghaudi I and II missiles, is a national hero in Pakistan, where his birthday is sanctified in mosques.[1] He is the only Pakistani to have received the highest civilian award of "Nishan-i-Imtiaz" twice—in 1996 and 1998.[2] "His stature is so elevated and protected by the Pakistani government," writes Dr. Rajesh Kumar Mishra of the South Asia Analysis Group, "that he has been epitomized as larger than the 'nuclear image' of Pakistan. Anything said or done against this scientist is considered to be anti-Pakistan, anti-Islam, and intolerable."[3]

In the United States and Europe, however, Dr. Khan is viewed as a rogue scientist, a nuclear madman, and an individual far more dangerous than Osama bin Laden or Saddam Hussein. "If the international community had a proliferation most wanted list, A. Q. Khan would be most wanted on the list," said Robert J. Einhorn, assistant secretary of state for the Clinton administration.[4]

Dr. Khan has responded to such criticism by saying: "All Western countries, including Israel, are not only the enemies of Pakistan but, in fact, of Islam. Had any other Muslim country instead of Pakistan made this progress, they would have conduced the same poisonous propaganda about it. The examples of Iraq and Libya are before you."[5]

Dr. Khan began his career by working for Urenco, a top-secret uranium enrichment plant in the Netherlands. Urenco perfected the technology for enriching uranium to weapons-grade strength in gas centrifuges. As far back as 1974, when India tested its first nuclear device, Khan stole the plans for uranium enrichment, fled the country, and set up his own nuclear testing facility—A. Q. Khan Research Laboratories—near Islamabad—where he began to build atomic bombs with the assistance of Chinese technicians and scientists.[6] In 1983, following an investigation into the alleged theft, an Amsterdam court sentenced Khan in absentia to four years in prison for attempted espionage.[7]

Much of the funding for Khan's laboratories in Pakistan purportedly came from Saudi Arabian businessmen who were anxious to see the development of "the Islamic bomb."[8] Because Pakistan was providing support for CIA covert activities in Afghanistan to ward off the Soviet invasion, the United States took no steps to thwart the clandestine development of the Islamic bomb until the testing took place during the Clinton administration.[9]

Several years before the unveiling of the Islamic bomb, Dr. Khan, at the request of Pakistan's former prime minister Benazir Bhutto, engaged in discussions with North Korean officials for the purchase of twelve to fourteen Nodong ballistic missiles for the Pakistani government. A deal was struck. In exchange for the six hundred-mile-range, nuclear-capable missiles that would be modified to produce the Ghaudis, Khan provided the Dutch blueprints for enriching uranium by gas centrifuges. The deal enabled North Korea to emerge as the most formidable nation in President Bush's infamous "axis of evil."[10] From 1998 to 2001, the esteemed scientist made more than thirteen separate trips to Pyongyang to consult with scientists and technicians at the Yongbyon Uranium Enrichment Plant. Khan also hosted a delegation of Pyongyang officials and scientists at his research laboratory in Pakistan.[11]

In 2001, Dr. Khan met with Iran's president Mohammad Khatami and offered to place the country's nuclear weapons program on the fast track by providing Iran with the same pilfered blueprints that he had used in Pakistan and delivered to North Korea. Within a matter of months, he reportedly implemented a program for the enrichment of uranium at the Bushehr Nuclear Power Plant and oversaw the construction of nuclear facilities in Arak and Natanz.[12] Iran, according to most estimates, is expected as a full-scale member of the nuclear club by 2005.[13] The situation provided significant impetus to President Bush in his decision to launch an invasion of Iraq in March 2003. Without toppling Saddam Hussein, propping up a friendly regime, and without establishing strategically located military bases throughout Iraq, the United States could not hope to contain the growing Iranian nuclear threat.[14]

Dr. Khan also offered his services to other Islamic countries. In an intercepted letter to Saddam Hussein, before the dictator was toppled from power, the Pakistani scientist made an offer "to establish a project to enrich uranium and manufacture a nuclear weapon for Iraq."[15] He made a similar offer to Libyan president Moammar Gaddafi.[16] At that point, Gadhafi accepted and Dr. Khan became the leading supplier of nuclear know-how to yet another Muslim nation.[17] Italian officials intercepted a shipment of centrifuge parts to Libya in October 2003.[18]

Commenting on Dr. Khan's title as "the godfather of nuclear proliferation," Robert Oakley, the former US ambassador to Pakistan, said: "I've always thought that A. Q. Khan's Rolodex is the most important thing of all in giving people advice on how to put all the pieces together."[19]

Even more alarming than the revered scientist's place within "the axis of evil" is his connection to Islamic terrorist groups. Khan has appeared in rallies and at conclaves of Lashkar-e-Toiba ("the Army of the Pure"), the officially banned terrorist arm of the Markaz Dawa-Wal-Irshad, an Islamic organization of the Wahhabi sects in Pakistan.[20] Wahhabi sects follow the radical teachings of eighteenth-century emir Abdul al-Wahhab. Bin Laden, al-Zawahiri, and all high-ranking al Qaeda officials are Wahhabists.

Lashkar-e-Toiba specialized in the mass murder of Hindus and was responsible for the following acts of terrorism: the slaughter of twenty-three people in Wandhama on January 23, 1988; the cold-blooded murder of twenty-five members of a wedding party in Doda on June 19, 1998; the Chattisinghpora massacre of March 20, 2000, in which thirty-five men, women, and children were hacked to pieces; and the November 24, 2002, attack of two Hindu shrines—the Raghunath and the Panjbakhtar temples in Jammu—that left thirteen dead and forty-five injured.[21] In 2003, Lashkar-e-Toiba changed its name to Jamaat-ud-Dawa and became the coordinating agency for pro–bin Laden networks throughout the world.[22] On February 2, 2002, Abu Zubeidah, a member of al Qaeda's *Shura*, or consultation council, was discovered hiding in a Lashkar-e-Toiba safe house in Faisalabad. Abu Zubaydah, a key strategist of 9/11, was the terror chief responsible for the instruction and dispatch of Richard Reid, the alleged "shoe bomber" who tried to blow up an American Airlines plane in December 2001.[23] At several Lashkar-e-Toiba rallies, Dr. Khan has appeared with other leading scientists from his research laboratory, including Sultan

Bashiruddin Mahmood, former director of Pakistan's Atomic Energy Commission.[24]

In November 2001, during the first phase of Operation Enduring Freedom, US military officials discovered records within a safe house in Kabul of meetings between scientists from the A. Q. Khan Research Laboratories, including Sultan Bashiruddin Mahmood, and several al Qaeda officials, including bin Laden and al-Zawahiri.[25] The discovery, according to the *Washington Post*, was so alarming that CIA director George Tenet immediately raced to Islamabad to investigate the matter.[26]

Sultan Bashiruddin Mahmood represented the perfect person to provide assistance in nuclear technology to al Qaeda. He had spent over twenty years working on the enrichment of uranium at the Khan Research Laboratories.[27] His expertise was so respected by his colleagues that in 1995 he was named chairman of the Pakistan Atomic Energy Commission. Before his retirement in 2001, Dr. Mahmood served as the head of the Khosab reactor in the Punjab region—a reactor that produces weapons-grade plutonium. On several public occasions, he stated his belief that plutonium production should not be a state secret and advocated increased plutonium production to help other Islamic nations build nuclear bombs for protection against Israel and the West.[28]

In addition to his hands-on technical expertise with nuclear weapons, Dr. Mahmood, like other executives at the Khan Research Laboratories, possessed an extensive knowledge of black market sources for fissile materials throughout the Middle East and Asia.[29] Much of the material to build the first atomic bomb came from these sources.

"Mahmood was one of the nuclear hawks," said Rifaat Hussain, the chairman of defense and strategic studies at Quaid-I-Azam University in Islamabad. "People say that he was a very capable scientist and very capable engineer, but he had this totally crazy mind-set."[30]

Proof of his crazy mind-set can be found in his writings. In *Mechanics of the Doomsday and Life after Death*, published in 1987, Dr. Mahmood maintained that natural catastrophes occur in places where moral degradation becomes rampant.[31] In *Cosmology and Human Destiny*, published two years later, he argued that sunspots determine the course of human events, including World War II, the revolution against colonial power in India, the Soviet invasion of Eastern Europe, and the rise of the *mujahadeen*.[32] In this latter work, he maintained that Pakistan's energy problems could be solved by finding a means of harnessing the energy emitted by *djinns*, the fairylike spirits who inhabit the world of Islam.[33]

In 1987, Dr. Mahmood founded the Holy Koran Research Foundation to incorporate the findings of science with the tenets of Islam. In 2001, he expressed his belief to members of the foundation that the US invasion of Afghanistan represented the beginning of "the last war between Islam and the infidels."[34]

On October 23, 2001, following the discovery of records concerning Dr. Mahmood's ties to al Qaeda within the safe house in Kabul, Pakistani Inter Service Intelligence (ISI) agents, at the behest of CIA director Tenet, arrested Dr. Mahmood at the headquarters of Ummah Tameer E-Nau (UTN) ("Islamic Reconstruction") in Afghanistan. UTN was a so-called charitable organization that Mahmood established "to serve the hungry and needy of Afghanistan."[35] When dragged before CIA interrogators, Dr. Mahmood denied that he had ever made contact with bin Laden. He acknowledged, however, that he had met with Mullah Mohammed Omar, the supreme leader of the Taliban, to discuss the building of a flour mill in Kabul to provide bread for the masses. Dr. Mahmood insisted that he knew bin Laden only by reputation as a fellow humanitarian who "was helping in different places, renovating schools, opening orphan houses and helping with the rehabilitation of widows."[36]

After months of questioning, Dr. Mahmood at last admitted that he had met bin Laden and other al Qaeda officials, including al-Zawahiri, in Kabul on several occasions, including two to three days in August 2001 and on the fateful morning of September 11. The purpose of the meetings, he confessed, was not to discuss the nutritional benefits of whole wheat bread but the benefits of an atomic blast in an American city.

Bin Laden, Dr. Mahmood told the interrogators, was in possession of fissile materials from the Islamic Movement of Uzbekistan and other sources and was seeking the means to speed up the process of manufacturing nukes for the *jihad*.[37]

Dr. Mahmood insisted that he had been pleased to provide academic answers to questions regarding nuclear technology, but insisted he had declined to provide technical assistance for bin Laden's nuclear project to recreate a Hiroshima blast in the United States.[38] Upon making this denial, Dr. Mahmood was subjected to six lie-detector tests. He failed them all.[39]

In November 2001, CIA officials conducted a search of UTN headquarters in Kabul and found large amounts of data on the construction and maintenance of nuclear weapons from the A. Q. Khan Research Laboratories, communiqués between UTN and Islamic terrorist groups (including Lashkar-e-Toiba), and documents outlining a plan to kidnap an American attaché.[40] They also discovered illustrations running the length of one room that showed how high-altitude balloons could be used to release large quantities of anthrax and bubonic plague bacilli over major metropolitan areas of the United States.[41]

In the wake of these discoveries, President Bush announced that his administration was working with US allies, including Pakistani president Musharraf, to freeze the financial assets of UTN. "UTN claims to serve the hungry and needy of Afghanistan," Bush said, "but it was UTN that provided information about nuclear weapons to al Qaeda. We're issuing orders to block any of their assets within US jurisdiction, and putting the world on notice that anyone who continues to do business with Islamic Reconstruction and its principal figures will not do business with the United States."[42]

At the same news conference, President Bush condemned Lashkar-e-Toiba (LAT), the terrorist group that numbered Dr. Khan and Dr. Mahmood among its most prominent members. "LAT is a stateless sponsor of terror, and it hopes to destroy relations between Pakistan and India and undermine Pakistani president Musharraf. LAT is a terrorist organization that presents a global threat, and I look forward to working with the governments of both India and Pakistan in a common effort to shut it down, and bring the killers to justice."[43]

While Dr. Mahmood remained under lock and key with guards watching over him twenty-four hours a day, US officials discovered that bin Laden had held clandestine meetings with a host of other Pakistani nuclear scientists. After being threatened with seven years in prison under Pakistan's Official Secrets Act, Dr. Chaudry Abdul Majid, a chief engineer for the Pakistan Atomic Energy Commission (PAEC), reportedly admitted that he had met with bin Laden and other al Qaeda officials to discuss the construction and maintenance of nuclear weapons.[44] Dr. Mirza Yusuf Baig, another engineer from PAEC, purportedly made a similar confession.[45] Dr. Mohammad Ali Mukhtar and Dr. Suleiman Asad, nuclear engineers and close colleagues of Dr. Khan and Dr. Mahmood, managed to slip out of Pakistan to Myanmar, reportedly to escape interrogation by US officials. Both scientists were believed to have met with bin Laden on numerous occasions.[46] Other senior nuclear engineers from the Khan Research Laboratories, who remain wanted for questioning, escaped from Pakistan for unknown destinations. The list of such "absconders" includes the names of Muhammad Zubair, Murad Qasim, Tariq Mahmood, Saeed Akhther, Imtaz Baig, Waheed Nasir, Munawar Ismail, Shaheen Fareed, and Khalid Mahmood.[47]

The interrogations, coupled with the findings from UTN's headquarters, seemed to verify for the CIA that al Qaeda had produced several nuclear weapons from highly enriched uranium and plutonium pellets the size of silver dollars. At least one weapon was smuggled out of Afghanistan before 9/11. The weapon was transported to Karachi, where it reportedly was shipped out to America in a cargo container.[48] These discoveries were alarming. There existed eighteen million potential delivery vehicles that could be used to bring a nuclear device into the United States. That is the number of cargo containers that arrive in the country annually. Of them, only 3 percent are inspected. Moreover, the bills of lading do not have to be produced until the containers reach their place of destination.[49]

In March 2003 the CIA also uncovered information concerning an earlier clandestine meeting between Dr. Khan and Khalid Shaikh Mohammed, the captured military leader of al Qaeda.[50] They also discovered that Khan and bin Laden had connections with the same safe house operator in Kabul and had been at "the same place at approximately the same time."[51]

At about the same time, intelligence sources reportedly amassed evidence that ISI officials allegedly executed American reporter Daniel Pearl because the journalist had obtained inside information on the close relationship between Dr. Khan and bin Laden, and on the trafficking of nuclear materials and know-how from Khan's facility near Islamabad to al Qaeda cells in the North-West Frontier Province.[52] In June 2003, Eliza Manningham-Butler, head of Britain's Security Service (MI5), blew her cover regarding such matters when she told an audience at the Royal United Services Institute in London: "We are faced with a realistic possibility of a form of unconventional attack that could include chemical, biological, radiological, and nuclear (CBRN) weapons. We know renegade scientists have cooperated with al Qaeda and provided them with some of the knowledge they need to develop these [nuclear] weapons. It is only a matter of time before a crude version of a CBRN is launched on a Western city and it is only a matter of time before the crude version becomes more sophisticated."[53]

Dr. Khan's possible role in the death of Daniel Pearl is supported by reports of others who have suffered misfortunes by probing into his activities. On June 9, 1998, one week after Pakistan's first nuclear tests, Kang Thae-yun, a North Korean diplomat, and Kim Sa-nae, his wife, were shot and killed in Islamabad. Kang Thae-yun allegedly was an international arms dealer who had been a supplier of nuclear materials to Khan, including maraging steel, a corrosion-resistant alloy used in warheads and a vital component for the enrichment of uranium. At the time of his death, Kang Thae-yun reportedly had been providing US intelligence sources with sensitive details of the Nodong missile deal between North Korea and Pakistan.[54] Much earlier, in July 1979, unidentified thugs stopped and severely beat the French ambassador to Pakistan and his first secretary as they were conducting a drive-by inspection of Khan's laboratories in Kahuta.[55] A few weeks later, Chris Sherwell, a journalist for the *Financial Times*, was beaten up by Khan security officials and later arrested on trumped-up charges by the ISI after seeking to locate Dr. Khan for an interview.[56]

In 2002, under growing US pressure, President Musharraf retired Dr. Khan as head of Pakistan's nuclear programs and appointed him as "special presidential advisor." Khan's demotion was decried by Nawaz Sharif, the former prime minister, as a hideous conspiracy designed to roll back the nuclear program and weaken the country's defenses.[57] Musharraf attempted to impart a soft spin to his decision by saying: "Nations cannot afford to sit on their laurels. Success must be reinforced. New ideas and new blood must be injected. I always believed that the time to make a transition is when you are on top. I also believe that transition must be effected smoothly so that there is no dislocation of objectives. Giving any other color and meaning to my decision is unfair."[58]

On February 4, 2004, Dr. Khan issued a public statement in which he confessed that he had sold blueprints for nuclear weapons to Libya, Iran, and North Korea. He expressed "the deepest sense of sorrow and anguish" that he had placed Pakistan's national security in jeopardy. "I have much to answer for it," he said.[59] Pakistan's Federal Cabinet and President Musharraf responded to this statement by granting Dr. Khan a full pardon for acts of proliferation. Musharraf said that Dr. Khan and the scientists who worked with him were motivated by "money."[60] The pardon, according to some observers, represented an attempt by the Musharraf government to appease Islamic extremists and senior Pakistani military officials who believe that Musharraf had become a traitor to the Muslim people by providing military support and assistance to the Bush administration.[61] The Pakistani president, however, agreed to restrict Dr. Khan's travel and to have two military officials accompany the public hero on his trips within the country.[62]

Concerns have also been raised over the security of the storage facilities for Pakistan's nuclear weaponry. At the start of the US bombing campaign, President Musharraf ordered an immediate redeployment of Pakistan's nuclear weapons to six secret locations.[63] The warheads are now kept separate from the missiles. The warheads remain equipped with electronic components and high explosives but are stripped of their fissile cores. The uranium and plutonium cores are about the size of watermelons, each weighing about sixty-six pounds. These cores have been broken down into components for separate storage. The different components are stored in different facilities.[64] For this reason, a terrorist group would not be able to break into a weapons facility and steal a fully mounted nuclear weapon. Nor could the group obtain all the separate parts from one location.

This system should serve to make the weapons more secure, but, as George Perkovich, a nuclear weapons expert at the W. Alton Jones Foundation points out, it also makes them highly movable for loading in a transport truck or helicopter, since the various parts have been methodically disassembled.[65] To be sure, Perkovich says, skilled technicians, familiar with the storage system, would be required to assemble the weapons and make them work. But Pakistan's community of nuclear scientists and technicians remains "profoundly fundamentalist" and anti-American.[66] They remain particularly resentful of the economic and military sanctions against Pakistan's nuclear weapons program that were imposed by the Bush administration following the discoveries of proliferation.[67] Such concerns give rise to the larger and more-pressing question: What will happen if the next assassination attempt against Musharraf proves successful and proponents of radical Islam seize control of the government and its "crown jewels?"

THE COMING NIGHTMARE

The premises on which we base ourselves as an organization, and on which we base our operations and our method of action, are practical and realistic. They are also scientific and in accordance with Islamic religious law, and they give us confidence and certainty. In writing them and in publicly revealing them, I do not intend to be apologetic for what was done; I lay these arguments before you so as to emphasize that we are continuing with our blows against the Americans and the Jews, and, with attacking them, both people and installations so as to stress that what awaits the Americans will not, Allah willing, be less than what has already happened to them. America must prepare itself; it must go to maximum alert; because, Allah willing, the blow will come from where they least expect it.

—Sulaiman Abu Ghaith, al Qaeda spokesman,
"Why We Fight America," June 12, 2002

Known members of al Qaeda on the FBI's Most Wanted Terrorists list

(More information on these individuals is available at
http://www.fbi.gov/mostwant/terrorists/fugitives.htm.)

Osama bin Laden

Ayman al-Zawahiri

Abdelkarim Hussein Mohamed al-Nasser

Abdullah Ahmed Abdullah

Muhsin Musa Matwalli Atwah

Ali Atwa

Anas al-Liby

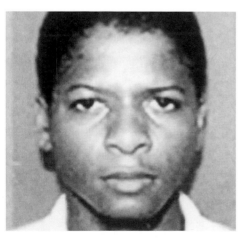

Ahmed Khalfan Ghailani

Hasan Izz-al-Din

Ahmed Mohammed Hamed Ali

Fazul Abdullah Mohammed

Imad Fayez Mugniyah

Mustafa Mohamed Fadhil

Sheikh Ahmed Salim Swedan

Abdul Rahman Yasin

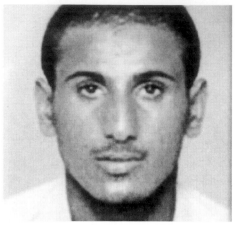

Fahid Mohammed Ally Msalam

Ahmad Ibrahim al-Mughassil

Muhammad Atef

Ali Saed bin Ali el-Hoorie

Saif al-Adel

Ibrahim Salih Mohammed al-Yacoub

CHAPTER 9

SLEEPING WITH THE ENEMY

Why was the world surprised? Why were millions of people astonished by what happened on September 11? Did the world think that anything else would happen? That something less than this would happen? What happened to America is something natural, an expected event for a country that uses terror, arrogant policy, and suppression against the nations and the peoples, and imposes a method, thought, and way of life, as if the people of the entire world are clerks in its government offices and employed by its commercial companies and institutions.

—Sulaiman Abu Ghaith,
"Why We Fight America," June 12, 2002

The confrontation that we are calling for with the apostate regimes does not know Socratic debates, Platonic ideals, or Aristotelian diplomacy. But it knows the dialogue of bullets, the ideals of assassination, bombing and destruction, and the diplomacy of the cannon and machine gun. Islamic governments have never and will never be established through peaceful solutions and cooperative councils. They are established, as they always have been, by pen and gun, by word and bullet, and by tongue and teeth.

—Al Qaeda Training Manual

I n his 2002 State of the Union address, President George W. Bush warned of al Qaeda sleeper cells by saying: "Thousands of dangerous killers, schooled in the methods of murder, often supported by outlaw regimes, are now spread throughout the world, set to go off without warning."[1] President Bush failed to add that up to five thousand sleeper agents were already in major US cities, including New York, Los Angeles, Las Vegas, Miami, Detroit, and Charlotte, North Carolina, preparing for "the American Hiroshima."[2]

These sleeper agents had been trained for special operations at al Qaeda camps in Afghanistan and Pakistan before 9/11. Most came from *madrassahs* throughout the Middle East (including the six thousand in Pakistan). Others were recruits from mosques and Muslim schools in Indonesia, Europe, and the United States. Typically, al Qaeda utilized the services of scouts (such as receptive teachers of Islamic studies at colleges and universities or the emirs at various mosques) to identify candidates suitable for training. The scouts found the Farouq Mosque in Brooklyn, New York, to be a particularly good breeding ground for future terrorists.[3] Most candidates were young men between the ages of eighteen and twenty-four who had been injured by ethnic conflict or who came from the lower echelons of society.[4]

At the training camps, recruits learned how to fire Russian-made Kalashnikov rifles, to pick planes out of the sky with surface-to-air missiles, and to pack plastic explosives in Samsonite suitcases. They also were subjected to intense religious training and compelled to commit long passages from the Koran to memory.[5] At the conclusion of six weeks of this "basic training," the recruits were compelled to take the *bayat* (the blood oath of allegiance) to Osama bin Laden.

Select recruits were then chosen for "special operations training" at one of al Qaeda's top-tier *jihad* camps, such as the Zahwar Kal al-Bar camp in the Kush Mountains. Here they were trained in intelligence management, kidnapping, hijacking, explosives, and methods of mass murder. The *Al Qaeda Training Manual*, a copy of which was found in Manchester, England, on May 10, 2000, outlined the following methods of psychological torture:

1. Isolate the victim socially, cutting him off from public life, placing him in solitary confinement, and denying him news and information in order to make him feel lonely.
2. Forbid calling him by name, giving the victim a number, and calling him that number in order to defeat his morale.
3. Threaten to summon his sister, mother, wife, or daughter and rape her.
4. Threaten to rape the victim himself.
5. Threaten to confiscate his possessions and to have him fired from his employment.
6. Threaten to cause him permanent physical disability or life imprisonment.
7. Offer the victim certain enticements (apartment, car, passport, scholarship, and so on).
8. Use harsh treatment, insults, and curses to defeat his morale.[6]

The manual maintained that the best places to stab victims or captives are in the following parts of the body: (1) the rib cage, (2) the eye, (3) the pelvis (under the navel), (4) the area above the genitals, (5) the axon (the back of the head), and (6) the base of the spinal column.[7] It went on to suggest the following methods of physical torture:

1. Blindfolding and the removal of all clothing
2. Hanging by the hands
3. Hanging by the feet
4. Beatings with sticks and electric wires
5. Putting out lighted cigarettes on the victim's skin
6. Shocking with electric currents
7. Making the victim sit on a sharp stake
8. Throwing the victim in a septic tank
9. Pulling out the nails and hair
10. Flooding the victim's cell with sewage
11. Giving the victim large quantities of water and watery fruits, such as watermelon, after denying him food and water for several days. After the victim drinks the water and eats the fruit, his hands and feet should be bound in such a way that the victim will be unable to urinate
12. Hitting the victim's genitals with a stick or squeezing them by hand
13. Dragging the victim over barbed wire and fragments of shattered glass[8]

Included in the manual were favorite al Qaeda recipes for poison from such ingredients as green and rotten potato sprouts (a source of deadly solanine), crushed cigarettes (three are sufficient to kill a troublesome soul within an hour), crushed castor beads (a source of ricin), and the sap of water hemlock plants, which, when injected into the blood stream, will cause such violent convulsions that most victims will bite their tongues.[9]

After weeks of Berlitz-style language training, the special-op recruits received training in standard security precautions and proper means of deportment while on a mission. The following guidelines were presented in the manual:

1. Keep the passport in a safe.
2. All documents of the undercover brother, such as identity cards and passports, should be falsified.
3. When the undercover brother is traveling with a certain identity card or passport, he should know all pertinent information, such as his name, profession, and place of residence.
4. The brother who has special work status (commander, communication link) should have more than one identity card or passport. He should learn the contents of each, the nature of the indicated profession, and the dialect of the resident area listed in the document.
5. The photograph of the brother in these documents should be without a beard. It is preferable that the brother's public photograph on these documents also be without a beard.
6. When using identity documents in different names, no more than one such document should be carried at one time.

The handy manual further stated a series of precautions that must be observed by all agents when eating, drinking, applying for employment, and hunting for living quarters within the lands of the *kafirs* (non-Muslims), such as Great Britain and the United States. It outlined the following guidelines for using public transportation:

1. One should select public transportation that is not subject to frequent checking along the way, such as crowded trains or public buses.
2. Boarding should be done at secondary stations, since main stations undergo more careful surveillance.
3. The cover should match the general appearance (tourist class, first class, second class, and so on).

4. The document used should support the cover.
5. Important luggage should be placed among the passengers' luggage without identification tags. If it is discovered, its owner would not be arrested.
6. The brother traveling on a "special mission" should not arrive in the destination country at night because then travelers are few and there are search parties and checkpoints along the way.
7. When cabs are used, conversation of any kind should not be started because many cab drivers work for security apparatus.
8. The brother should exercise extreme caution and apply all security measures to the other members.[10]

In addition to the above, the manual stated tried-and-true methods of appearing like the "polytheists" in Europe and the United States in order to avert suspicion. The methods ranged from carrying rosary beads in a pocket to taking an unbeliever as a wife. Other helpful hints included the following:

1. Never reveal your true name to cell members or associates at your place of employment.
2. Have a general appearance that does not indicate Islamic orientation, such as a beard, a long shirt, or even a toothpick.
3. Never visit Islamic places, not even the local mosque.
4. Maintain friendly relationships with family members (if married to a *kafir*) and neighbors.
5. Never speak loudly.
6. Never get involved in advocating good or denouncing evil.
7. Never park in a no-parking zone or take photographs where it is forbidden.

8. Never undergo a change in your daily routine.
9. Never talk to your wife about *jihad* work.[11]

The closing sections of the terror manual contained the following instructions regarding the selection of a proper place to store weapons of mass destruction, including, presumably, the nuclear suitcase bombs:

1. The arsenal should not be in a well-protected area or close to parks or public places.
2. The arsenal should not be in "no-man's-land."
3. The arsenal should not be in an apartment previously used for suspicious activities.
4. The place selected should be purchased by the agent or rented on a long-term basis.
5. The brother responsible for storage should not visit the arsenal frequently nor toy with the weapons.
6. Only the weapons keeper and the commander should know the location of the arsenal.[12]

Although President Bush sounded the alarm about the presence of al Qaeda operatives in the United States, federal officials have displayed almost total incompetence in their ability to identify sleeper agents and root out sleeper cells. This incompetence became most apparent in the case of Ali Abdelsoud Mohamed.

Ali Abdelsoud Mohamed joined the Egyptian army in 1971, rising to the rank of major by 1980. While still in the army, he secretly joined Egypt's Islamic Jihad, the group responsible for the assassination of President Anwar Sadat in 1981. In 1984, Mohamed was dismissed from the military on the suspicion that he had become a religious and political fanatic.[13]

In 1985 he married an American woman, became a US citizen, and settled in California's Silicon Valley. Within the year, he enlisted in the US Army and was granted the rank, based on his previous military experience, of supply sergeant.[14]

In 1991 he was recruited for the *jihad* by members of the Al-Kifah Refugee Center in Brooklyn, New York, an agency that served as a front for al Qaeda. He was sent to Sudan to assist bin Laden in establishing a base of operations and to train al Qaeda operatives in intelligence techniques and the proper means of detonating explosive devices.[15]

When he returned to the United States, Ali Mohamed brought al-Zawahiri with him to launch a fund-raising campaign for the *mujahadeen*.[16] At the same time, he became closely involved with Sheik Omar Abdel Rahman, the fiery one-eyed imam who would be responsible for the assassination of Rabbi Meir Kahane in New York and the bombing of the World Trade Center in 1993.[17]

In 1993 the FBI questioned Mohamed after his identification was found on an al Qaeda agent who was attempting to enter the United States from Vancouver. During the interview, Mohamed openly admitted that he was a member of bin Laden's terrorist group and that he had trained hundreds of al Qaeda operatives at training camps in Sudan. Despite this startling admission, the FBI released Mohamed from custody because he failed one lie-detector test.[18]

Upon his release, Mohamed made several trips to Kenya and Tanzania to assist fellow al Qaeda operatives in planning the bombing of the US embassies. He also traveled to Afghanistan to help train new recruits.

On August 8, 1998, one day after the bombings of the embassies in Kenya and Tanzania, FBI officials arrested Mohamed at his home in Sacramento, California, with a warrant from a special judge under the Foreign Intelligence Surveillance Act. Within Mohamed's residence, the officials discovered instructions and charts for blowing up buildings and bridges, and encoded messages regarding al Qaeda's plans for the future.[19]

After pleading guilty to his crimes, Mohamed told federal officials that their current profiles of sleeper agents were "invalid."[20]

Ali Mohamed's case represents merely one example of the failure of US intelligence officials to identify sleeper agents—even when such agents appear before them. "For five years, he [Ali Mohamed] was moving back and forth between the United States and Afghanistan," said Nabil Sharef, a former Egyptian intelligence officer. "It's impossible the CIA thought he was going there as a tourist. If the CIA hadn't caught on to him, it should be dissolved, and its budget used for something worthwhile."[21]

The national news media in the United States has shown itself to be equally inept at spotting sleepers. In 1998, ABC News employed Tarik Hamdi of Herndon, Virginia, to help secure an interview with bin Laden. The network transported Hamdi to Afghanistan, unaware that his real purpose in going there, according to informed sources, was to convey a replacement battery to bin Laden for his satellite telephone, which he would later use to orchestrate the embassy bombings.[22]

The sleeper agents, who are now among the American people, could be married to non-Muslims and living in spacious houses in the suburbs, or they could be single and living in inner-city apartment complexes. They could be attending Christian worship services on Sunday mornings and working as professionals at schools, hospitals, research facilities, chemical plants, nuclear energy facilities, and even government offices. Some, like Ali Abdelsoud Mohamed, might be serving in the armed forces. Others, like Tarik Hamdi, might be working for national news agencies. They could be living exemplary lives, according to Islamic precepts, by abstaining from premarital sex, liquor, drugs, and tobacco. Or else they might be individuals with a weakness for Camel cigarettes and various intoxicants, along with a taste for pornography and prostitutes. The al Qaeda terrorist who attempted to fly a plane into the fifty-five-story Rialto Towers, Australia's highest building, was a frequent customer at the Main Course brothel in downtown Melbourne, where he became notorious "as a bit of a sneak, always trying to get more than he paid for."[23]

In January 2004, when federal officials set out to identify and locate the two thousand to five thousand sleeper agents at work within the United States, the doomsday clock, the symbol of nuclear danger, read seven minutes to midnight.[24]

CHAPTER 10

BEHOLD A PALE HORSE

When the Lamb opened the fourth seal, I heard the voice of the fourth living creature say, "Behold!" I beheld and there before me was a pale horse! Its rider was Death and Hades was following close behind him.

—Revelation 6:8–9

Senator James Inhofe (R-OK)—*I do agree about the threat, the terrorist threat that's here, the suitcases. No one from Oklahoma has to be told what that threat is. And the devastation of the Murrah Federal Office Building was the explosive power of one ton of TNT; the smallest nuclear warhead we really heard about is about a kiloton, a thousand times that destruction. So I would hope we do not get ourselves into the position of saying we are either going to guard against terrorist attacks carrying suitcases or ICBMs, but not both; we need to have adequate protection against both of them.*

Secretary of Defense Donald Rumsfeld—*Well, senator, first let me say that I agree completely with you on the variety of the weapons of mass destruction and that it's important that we address the spectrum of them and not one and ignore others.*

—Testimony before the Senate Armed Forces Committee,
June 21, 2001

Where did they get this weapon? Where did they get the material from which it could have been made? Well, my list, and I believe that anybody at a meeting at the Defense Department or the White House would have a similar list absent specific evidence: Russia, Russia, Russia, Russia, Russia. The first five slots. Maybe they even deserve more, given the amount of material that's there.
—Dr. Graham Allison, Harvard University's Belfer Center for Science and International Affairs, February 20, 2003

W hy haven't Osama and the terrorists deployed his weapons of mass destruction yet? It seems that one attack should succeed another just as the invasion of Afghanistan gave way to the invasion of Iraq. But in the years since the attack on 9/11, Americans have watched and waited as the terror alert level rose and fell only to rise and fall again. Yet nothing happened. This is not to say that al Qaeda was becoming passive or inactive or vanquished. Quite to the contrary, new terrorist activities, as enumerated in chapter 7 of this book, have continued to escalate since the launching of Operation Enduring Freedom. But the big attack— the nuclear attack—that was supposed to come on New Year's Eve or at the Super Bowl or the political conventions never occurred. Many began to think that it would never occur—that America remained safe and secure under the new measures adopted by Homeland Security. Life returned almost to normal. By 2004, the national economy was on an upswing. Books on al Qaeda and bin Laden began to gather dust on the shelves of bookstores. Many Americans began to think that the coalition forces had managed to contain, if not capture, bin Laden and to thwart his grandiose plans for "an American Hiroshima."

Such speculation, unfortunately, fails to come to terms with the fact that one of bin Laden's defining characteristics is *patience*.[1] He started plotting the 1998 bombing of the US embassy in Kenya when he was in Sudan in 1993; the attack on the USS *Cole* was more than two years in the making; and ten years passed between the first attack on the World Trade Center and the second.[2] Bin Laden concluded his 1996 "Declaration of War against the Americans Occupying the Land of the Two Holy Places" with this prayer for patience: "Our Lord, make the youths of Islam steadfast and descend patience upon them and guide their shots. Our Lord, unify the Muslims and bestow love among their hearts! Our Lord, pour down upon us patience, make our steps firm, and assist us against the unbelieving people!" At al Qaeda training camps, recruits are instructed to repeat this passage from the Koran throughout the day: "I will be patient until Patience is worn out from patience."[3]

Still, the delay has caused many to wonder. Lt. Gen. Igor Volynkin, head of the Russian ministry's Twelfth Main Directorate, the agency responsible for the storage and security of nuclear weapons, argued that the delay reflects the fact that al Qaeda lacks the expertise to maintain, let alone detonate, the suitcase bombs and dirty nuclear devices in its possession. Valynkin said that the weapons must be disassembled every three months so that the nuclear cores can be recharged.[4]

Some American physicists disagree with this claim. They argue that the suitcases, most likely, are uranium or plutonium explosive devices, possibly based with tritium to compensate for the reduced amount of conventional explosive that would be needed to compress the fissile core in the compact device. Neither the uranium nor the plutonium would require frequent maintenance. Moreover, tritium has a half-life of 12.5 years. Such physicists point out that the United States has maintained a stockpile of similar nuclear weapons for over twenty years without the need of constant maintenance.[5]

Nonetheless, these physicists concur, the weapons would require constant maintenance and periodic overhauling. Most definitely, the "triggers," which emit large quantities of neutrons at high speeds, would require considerable attention. The triggers decay rapidly and have short "half-lives"—most would become useless in less than four months. The nuclear cores also are subject to decay and over the course of several years would fall below the critical mass threshold. Though the shells that encase the cores are the most durable, they, too, are subject to contamination. Without proper care, the shells, no less than the core, will produce a fizzle rather than a boom. But bin Laden has displayed a keen awareness of the need for technical expertise. Intelligence sources have confirmed that SPETSNAZ officials from the former Soviet Union were on bin Laden's payroll from 1996 to 2001 to maintain and prepare the nuclear suitcases for activation. Moreover, following the invasion of Afghanistan and the loss of his laboratories, bin Laden reportedly sought out and obtained the technical assistance of twelve leading Pakistani scientists, including Dr. Sultan Bashiruddin Mahmood, Dr. Chaudry Abdul Majid, and Dr. Mirza Yusuf Baig.[6] On November 25, 2001, Taliban leader Mullah Mohammed Omar assured BBC reporters that the nuclear destruction of the United States was well underway: "The plan is going ahead and, God willing, it is being implemented. But it is a huge task, which is beyond the will and comprehension of human beings. If God's help is with us, this will happen within a short period of time; keep in mind this prediction."[7]

The next attack, according to al Qaeda defectors and informants, will take place simultaneously at various locations throughout the country. Terrorist cells have been established in major American cities, including New York, Miami, Chicago, Las Vegas, Los Angeles, Detroit, and Washington, DC. Intelligence sources estimate that as many as five thousand sleeper agents from al Qaeda training camps have made their way into the country.[8]

Dr. Graham Allison, Harvard University's nonproliferation

expert, said that American people must face the fact that they are no longer safe—that al Qaeda and the radical Muslim Brotherhood is planning an event that places every man, woman, and child in jeopardy. "I think the difficult thing for us all to come to grips with is, my God, would people really want to kill thousands or tens of thousands of Americans?" Allison said.[9]

To assess the probability, if not the imminence, of the next attack, Dr. Allison said, one should adopt the investigative methodology of Sherlock Holmes in solving a crime or uncovering a potential crime—a methodology called "the MMO," for motive, means, and opportunity.

THE MOTIVE

In his fatwas, bin Laden said that America must be destroyed because of the presence of military bases in the Arabian Peninsula, the continual support of Israel, the Persian Gulf War of 1990, the deaths of over a million Iraqis (including 500,000 children by UN estimates) as a result of the economic sanctions imposed against Iraq, and the attempt to fragment the nations of Iraq, Saudi Arabia, Egypt, and Sudan into "paper statelets" of the United States. These outrages of oppression, political and economic division, and mass murder, bin Laden maintained, amounted to one thing: "a declaration of war on God, his messenger, and Muslims." The response for all believing Muslims, he proclaimed, must be clear-cut and decisive: "The ruling to kill Americans and their allies—civilians and military—is an individual duty of every Muslim who can do it in any country in which it is possible to do it, in order to liberate the Al-Aqsa Mosque and the holy mosque in Mecca from their grip, and in order for their armies to move out of all the lands of Islam, defeated and unable to threaten any Muslim."[10]

In an article entitled "Why We Fight America," Sulaiman Abu Ghaith, bin Laden's press secretary, argues that the *jihad* against the United States represents a defensive war that must be undertaken by all of Islam to ward off American aggression and to retaliate against the murders of millions of Muslims. He writes:

> America is the reason for all oppression, injustice, licentiousness, or suppression that is the Muslims' lot. It stands behind all the disasters that were caused and are being caused to the Muslims; it is immersed in the blood of Muslims and cannot hide this. . . . For 50 years in Palestine, the Jews—with the blessing and support of the Americans—carried out abominations of murder, suppression, abuse, and exile. The Jews exiled nearly 6.6 million Palestinians and killed nearly 260,000. They wounded nearly 180,000 and crippled nearly 160,000. . . . Due to the American bombings and siege of Iraq, more than 1,200,000 Muslims were killed in the past decade. . . . In its war with the Taliban and al Qaeda, America has killed 12,000 Afghan civilians and 350 Arab Jihad fighters, among them women and children. It annihilated entire families from among the Arab Jihad fighters while they were in their cars, when the American Air Force bombed them with helicopters and antitank missiles, until nothing remained except the body parts.[11]

Abu Ghaith goes on to say that the Islamic world must achieve "parity" with the United States for this loss of life. This belief justifies the following conclusion: "We have the right to kill four million Americans—two million of them children—and to exile twice as many and wound and cripple hundreds of thousands."[12]

THE MEANS

In 1993 bin Laden began his search to build a nuclear arsenal by attempting to purchase highly enriched uranium out of South Africa—a country that had a nuclear program under its previous government.[13] The search culminated in the purchase of forty-eight nuclear suitcases from the Russian Mafia, along with twenty kilos of uranium-236 from Semion Mogilevich, a Ukrainian arms dealers, and enough radioactive material from such black market sources in Russia, China, Kazakstan, and the Ukraine to build a multitude of dirty nukes. This finding has been affirmed by US, British, Pakistani, Saudi, and Israeli intelligence.[14] In November 2001, bin Laden told Hamid Mir, the editor of *Dawn*, the Pakistani daily newspaper: "We have chemical and nuclear weapons. It is not difficult [to obtain such weapons], not if you have contacts in Russia with other militant [Islamic] groups. They are available for $10 million and $20 million."[15]

Apocalyptic fears became intensified on September 14, 2001, when Israeli security arrested an al Qaeda operative as he attempted to enter Israel through Palestinian territories at a border checkpoint in Ramallah.[16] Concerning the arrest, one government official said: "There was only one individual involved. He was from Pakistan."[17] The Pakistani terrorist was carrying a radioactive backpack bomb—not one of the suitcases—a sophisticated weapon encased in plutonium that could have wreaked havoc throughout Israel. News of the nuke was conveyed to the state department and the weapon became listed in the CIA Daily Treat Report. The incident left no doubt that al Qaeda and other Islamic terrorist groups not only possessed nuclear weapons but also were ready to use them.[18]

The arrest of the Pakistani with the portable nuke was kept from the American public. The sealed-lips mentality in part reflected the prevailing belief of President Bush and White House officials that sounding an impending alarm would serve no beneficial purpose and might serve to weaken the struggling economy. This belief was evident shortly after 9/11, when the Bush administration opted to keep a tight lid on intelligence reports that al Qaeda operatives had obtained a ten-kiloton nuclear weapon from the Russian arsenal and were planning to smuggle it into New York City. These reports, which later were shown to be false, were not only kept from the national media but also from Mayor Rudolph Giuliani, the New York Police Department, and FBI officials.[19] New York City could have been reduced to a pile of burning cinders and no one—not even the mayor—would have been aware of the immediacy of nuclear disaster.

THE OPPORTUNITY

Granted that bin Laden has the motive and the means, he lacks only the opportunity, and such an opportunity would remain contingent upon the successful exportation of nuclear weapons from Pakistan to American soil. Mounting evidence shows that this objective already has been achieved.

On October 11, 2001, George Tenet, director of the Central Intelligence Agency, met with President Bush to present news that at least two nuclear suitcases have reached al Qaeda operatives in the United States. The news was substantiated by Pakistan's ISI (Inter Service Intelligence), the Central Intelligence Agency, and the Federal Bureau of Investigation. Each suitcase weighs eight kilograms and contains at least two kilotons of fissionable plutonium and uranium. One suitcase bears the serial number 9999 and Russian manufacturing date of 1988.[20] The design of the suitcases, Tenet told the president, is simple. The plutonium and uranium are kept in separate compartments that are linked to a triggering mechanism that can be activated by a clock or a call from a cell phone.[21]

The briefing raised fears that sent the president "through the roof," causing him to order his national security team to give nuclear terrorism priority over every other threat to America.[22]

Such fears also caused President Bush's activation of nuclear contingency plans—the first since the dawning of the Cold War—for the installation of underground bunkers away from major metropolitan areas so that a cadre of federal managers can proceed with the business of government if and when the nuclear attacks occur.[23]

In accordance with this finding, the Bush administration deployed hundreds of new and highly sophisticated Gamma Ray Neutron Flux Detector sensors to US borders, overseas facilities, and "choke points" around Washington, DC, to detect the presence of radioactive weapons.[24] The administration further assigned Delta Force, the elite special operations detachment unit of the US Army, the task of killing or disabling any and all suspects.

To beef up security and prevent more nukes from arriving, federal authorities began investigating all suspicious cash rentals of trucks and leases of small aircraft, including flight plans, since a small nuke could be dropped by terrorists via parachutes into remote areas of the country for retrieval by awaiting cell members. Airfreight suddenly appeared vulnerable since less than 25 percent of the freight carried by private planes is ever inspected.[25]

Federal officials also considered the possibility that suitcases could be placed aboard commercial jets, with carefully adjusted barometric detonators rigged to go off upon take off or landing and called for increased security for all major airports.

But the most nagging fear was that the weapons arrived or would arrive by ship, since the United States, even in times of high security alert, possessed "zip port security."[26] Bin Laden, officials knew, owned more than twenty-three ships and maintained close ties with many international shipping firms, including Saudi firms and firms controlled by the Sicilian Mafia, his former partners in the drug trafficking business. The open seas represented the easiest way to transport deadly cargo—including well-packed crates of small atomic demolition munitions—into the United States.

Regarding the possibility of nukes arriving by ship, Stephen Flynn, senior fellow for national security studies at the US Council of Foreign Relations, said: "The United States has 16,000 ships entering its ports every day. Adding in shipments entering by truck, train or air freight, the total number of import shipments to the US is 21.4 million tons a year. You could put a nuclear or chemical weapon aboard a ship leaving Karachi, and that ship will land at Vancouver, Oakland, San Francisco, or the Gulf Coast and we would never know the difference." Flynn said that less than 3 percent of ship containers ever get inspected—even the containers of ships arriving from the Middle East.[27]

Because of this concern, the *Palermo Senator*, a container vessel, was detained and searched at sea for four days after radiation traces were detected in its hold. The search was conducted after FBI officials received tips that forty al Qaeda agents were heading for Santa Catalina, an island several miles off the coast of Los Angeles. Nuclear weapons were not found, and the cause of the radiation was never detected. This incident, reports of which did not appear in national news outlets, would account for the reason why Vice President Dick Cheney was confined to a secure nuclear facility on September 9, 2002.[28]

But such frantic efforts might prove too little, too late. On January 7, 1998, Shaykh Hisham Kabbani, chairman of the Islamic Supreme Council of America, testified before a committee of the US Department of State that more than twenty nuclear warheads carried in suitcases have arrived in the United States and that more than five thousand suicide bombers have been trained for the next attack.[29] His statements are supported by Pakistani and Israeli intelligence.

In the same address, Kabbani also expressed *his* belief that 80 percent of the mosques in America have been taken over by Muslim extremists who are committed to the destruction of the United States.[30] The Muslim leader went on to say that Muslim schools, youth groups, community centers, political organizations, professional associations, and commercial enterprises within the United States share the views of Islamic militant groups, such as al Qaeda, and remain extremely hostile to American culture, wanting to replace it with an Islamic order.[31]

Shaykh Kabbani restated these claims, including his insistence that twenty nuclear suitcases have arrived in America, to members of the press in the wake of September 11, 2001.[32]

When will it happen? Al Qaeda, according to US military analysts, places a great deal of significance on dates. The bombing of the World Trade Center on February 26, 1993, was meant to coincide with the second anniversary of the beginning of the ground war in Operation Desert Storm on February 23, 1991. The date of 9/11 was significant to the Muslim terrorists because it represented the fifth anniversary of the conviction in a New York court of the World Trade Center bomber Ramzi Yousef on charges of criminal conspiracy. And the al Qaeda bombing of the US embassies in Nairobi, Kenya, and Dar es Salaam, Tanzania, took place on August 7, 1998, the eighth anniversary of President George H. W. Bush's 1990 commitment to send US troops to protect Saudi Arabia.

Some analysts believe that the favored month for the next attack is October. October 2 looms ominous, since it is the anniversary of the federal court conviction of blind Sheikh Omar Abdel Rahman, the spiritual mentor of bin Laden and Ayman al-Zawahiri. The ideal date, according to some intelligence sources, seems to be October 7, the day on which the United States began the attack on the Taliban and al Qaeda forces in Afghanistan.[33]

But such attempts to pinpoint a date are pure conjecture. In the mind of bin Laden, dates from the far-distant past remain as relevant as events that occurred in recent history—the Christian conquest of Jerusalem in 1099 remains an offense as outrageous as the US-led invasion of Iraq in 2003.[34] For this reason, the day for the next attack could be November 27, the day Pope Urban II launched the first crusade before a gathering of Christian knights at a field in Clermont in 1095. Therefore, pinpointing a date, without strong intelligence, represents an impossible task.

And how serious is the threat? "It's the most dangerous threat we face," says Ambassador Thomas Graham, who served as President Clinton's Special Representative for Nonproliferation and Disarmament. "We can find a way to deal with biological terror. But if these guys acquire enough nuclear weapons and blow up major cities, it wouldn't end civilization as we know it, but it would come pretty close."[35]

CHAPTER 11

WHAT WILL HAPPEN

"Is nuclear mega-terrorism inevitable"? Harvard professors are known for being subtle or ambiguous, but I'll try to be clear. "Is the worst yet to come?" My answer: Bet on it. Yes.

—Dr. Graham Allison, director, Harvard University's Belfer Center for Science and International Affairs, February 20, 2003

It's not a matter of if; it's a matter of when.

—Gen. Eugene E. Habiger,
former executive chief of US Strategic Weapons

Wait, our friends, salvation is at hand and the painful blow is on its way. It will be a sweeping attack recognizable, with God's help, to those who believe with all their hearts in jihad *and the* Mujahadeen. . . . *Praise Allah, the message of the sheikh has reached the general leadership of the Muslims and* Mujahadeen *throughout the world, and those orders will be understood only by those who are part of the* Mujahadeen. . . . *And wait, salvation is near and the painful blow is on the way. It will be sweeping, and with God's help and signs recognized by those who believe in their hearts in* jihad *and the* Mujahadeen. *And God will proclaim paradise and our sheikh will take the Islamic army to his bosom and its flag shall fly everywhere in the world. We are waiting.*

—Abu al-Bara'a al-Qarshy,
bin Laden's planning lieutenant, November 2003

PART THREE: THE COMING NIGHTMARE

The threat environment we face is as bad as it was before September 11. It is serious. They have reconstituted. They are coming after us.

—George Tenet, director of the CIA,
October 2002

The frightening possibility of nuclear weapons in the hands of a group of madmen has been in the public mind ever since the publication in 1993 of John McPhee's *The Curve of Binding Energy*. The book centered on the life and work of Theodore Taylor, the prominent American physicist who miniaturized the atomic bomb and designed the largest-yield fission bomb that has ever been exploded.

In contrast to the prevailing opinion among scientists, Taylor argued that it would not require a Manhattan Project effort to produce an atomic bomb. He pointed out that if a group of madmen could acquire fissile materials—such as highly enriched uranium or plutonium—from black market sources, it would be relatively easy and inexpensive for them, with the aid of several skilled technicians, to create a weapon with the same destructive capacity as the bomb dropped on Hiroshima. Step-by-step instructions for the building of such a bomb, Taylor said, were available at most public libraries.

In the closing chapter of *The Curve of Binding Energy*, McPhee recounts that Taylor took him to the World Trade Center towers to illustrate the devastating effects of a nuclear explosion in lower Manhattan. The author recalls that they entered the west tower, took the elevator to the fortieth floor, and walked to a window of the eastern wall. Surveying the city, Taylor said: "Through free air, a kiloton bomb would send a lethal dose of immediate radiation up to half a mile, or, up to a thousand feet, you'd be killed by projectiles. Anyone in an office facing the Trade Center would die."[1]

Taylor directed McPhee's attention across a space of six hundred feet, past the second tower, to a neighboring building at 1 Liberty Plaza, and said: "People in that building over there would get it in every conceivable way. Gamma rays would get them first. Next comes visible light. Next the neutrons. Then the air shock. Then missiles. Unvaporized concrete would go out of here at the speed of a rifle shot. A steel-and-concrete missile flux would go out one mile and would include in all maybe a tenth the weight of the building, about five thousand tons."[2]

Pointing to the plaza between the towers, Taylor said: "If you exploded a bomb down there, you could conceivably wind up with the World Trade Center's two buildings leaning against each other and still standing." He added: "There's no question at all that if someone were to place a half-kiloton bomb on the front steps where we came in, the building would fall in the river."[3]

The words of Theodore Taylor to John McPhee remain not only compelling but also truly prophetic. Yet the nightmare that Taylor imagined from the detonation of a dirty nuke with an explosive yield of a half-kiloton would pale in comparison with the real horrors that would be unleashed by a weapon from bin Laden's nuclear arsenal.

A nuclear explosion is more than a simple bomb blast. It consists of four deadly components: an air-pressure shock wave, both thermal and nuclear radiation, and radioactive fallout. The effects of such a disaster in a city such as New York, Los Angeles, or Washington, DC, would be cataclysmic. The air-pressure shock wave from a suitcase bomb with an explosive yield of ten kilotons would destroy everything in its path, even heavily reinforced steel-and-concrete buildings.[4]

Such an explosion would also emit intense thermal radiation, creating a fireball with a diameter that would expand to 460 feet. The core of the fireball would reach a maximum temperature of ten million degrees Celsius.[5] The enormity of this heat can only be realized when one notes that the heat within the World Trade Center towers never exceeded five thousand degrees Celsius. Metallic objects within 450 feet of ground zero would vaporize. At fourteen hundred feet from the blast, rubber and plastic objects would ignite and melt, and wooden structures would erupt in flames.[6]

The bomb would expend 35 percent of its energy in the form of this radiated heat. An additional 50 percent would be absorbed into the atmosphere to become a juggernaut blast—a wave ripping through the city at 670 miles per hour.[7] The buildings that survived the melting heat would be twisted like pretzels by the force of the incredible wind. No one within 740 feet of the blast could hope to survive—not even those locked in concrete cells within steel buildings.[8]

Within minutes, everything within three square miles would be destroyed. Over three hundred thousand people would die instantly.[9] Five hundred thousand or more would suffer severe burns and permanent blindness. Two to three hundred thousand more people would be killed and injured by the deadly hail of debris and shattered glass.[10]

If such a bomb had been detonated on September 11, 2001, the World Trade Center towers, all of Wall Street and the financial district, along with the lower tip of Manhattan up to Gramercy Park, and much of midtown, including the theater district, would lay in ruins.[11]

The survivors of the initial blast would be exposed to intense bursts of ionizing radiation that would devastate their immune systems. Half of those exposed to this gamma ray burst in excess of four hundred Rads would die of radiation poisoning within a matter of days.[12]

Next would come the fallout. The nuclear explosion would create a huge mushroom cloud of irradiated debris that would rise two to three miles in the air and then, forty minutes later, highly lethal fallout would begin to fall back to earth, showering the injured survivors and dooming the rescue workers. The dustlike contamination, under ordinary weather conditions, would ride for five to ten miles on prevailing winds, deep into the Bronx or Queens or New Jersey.[13] Up to 50 percent of the exposed population would die of radiation poisoning within subsequent weeks and months.

In the wake of such a disaster, New York would become an uninhabited wasteland. The radioactive buildings and streets would have to be demolished and the contaminated debris and topsoil removed. But irregular radiation patterns and hot spots would persist for hundreds, if not thousands, of years.[14]

Even the effects of the smallest of tactical nuclear bombs—a device with an explosive yield of one kiloton—would be nightmarish almost beyond comprehension. If such a weapon were detonated in Times Square, the blast and searing heat would gut buildings for two blocks in every direction, melting pedestrians and crushing workers at their desks.[15] Twenty to thirty thousand would be dead within seconds. The fireball created by the blast would travel more than a quarter mile, incinerating nearly everything and everybody in its path. The few survivors would die of radiation poisoning and third-degree burns within a day. The toll from this effect would exceed 250,000 people on any given day. Half a mile from the explosion, up at Rockefeller Center and down at Macy's, the exposed people would suffer a slower and more agonizing form of death.[16] By conservative estimates, millions would die; millions more would be left permanently blind, burned beyond recognition, and badly crippled.

There would be countless other effects to such an attack. The financial and cultural center of America would cease to exist. The GNP would drop more than 3 percent in a matter of seconds.[17] One of America's major ports would be closed indefinitely. Millions of people throughout the country would lose their jobs. At the same time, the vast number of wounded and traumatized victims would create an unprecedented health care crisis. Makeshift hospitals would be set up in schools, museums, libraries, and other public buildings, where many would languish without proper medical care. Populations would desert major urban areas. The process of commerce would come to a halt.[18] Within hours, America (along with a host of other industrialized countries) would fall into a deep depression from which there might be little chance of recovery.

The above represents an assessment of what would happen in New York during the next 9/11, and it's a small part of the picture. Bin Laden and members of al Qaeda's *Shura*, or consultation council, are planning to bomb several strategic places within the United States at the same time—in much the same way that they orchestrated the four-prong attack of 9/11. What might take place in New York could take place not only in cities such as Boston, Philadelphia, Miami, Chicago, Detroit, Las Vegas, Los Angeles, Houston, Portland, and Washington, DC, but also obscure locations such as Rappahannock, a rural Virginia county with high-level US intelligence premises, and Valdez, Alaska, where tankers load oil from the Trans-Alaska pipeline.[19]

"The best reason for thinking that it won't happen," Bill Keller wrote in his *New York Times* think piece about al Qaeda's plans to nuke the United States, "is that it hasn't happened yet—and that is terrible logic. The problem is not so much that we are not doing enough to prevent a terrorist from turning our atomic knowledge against us (although we are not). The problem is that there may be no such thing as 'enough.'"[20]

Saad al-Fagih, a Saudi dissident and al Qaeda insider, told a *Time* reporter that bin Laden now speaks with "strange confidence" about the next attack against America. "Before 9/11," al-Fagih said, "bin Laden would talk in general terms about a major attack coming and a major, major attack following. He [bin Laden] would say, 'The first attack is going to be this size,' pointing to the tip of his finger, and, 'The next is going to be this size,' indicating the whole length of his finger."[21]

EPILOGUE

When the earth convulses in her shock, and the earth disgorges her burdens, and the people say, "What is wrong with her?" that day she will tell her news that your Lord has inspired her. On that day, humankind will go forth divided to be shown their works. Thus whoever has done an atom of good will see it. And whoever has done an atom of evil will see it.

—"The Shock," Koran 1–8

The Calamity! What is the Calamity, and what will convey to you what the Calamity is? A day when humankind will be scattered like moths, and the mountains like carded wood. And for those whose balance is heavy, they will be in a contented life; and as for those whose balance is light, their place will be an abyss. And what will convey to you what it is? A raging fire.

—"The Calamity," Koran 1–11

He lives in a small village in Pakistan. He is tall—over 6'6"—and incredibly thin—less than 150 pounds. Although he was born in 1957 and remains relatively young, he appears to be very old. His long scraggly beard is pure white; his face is lined with countless wrinkles; and his shoulders are hunched and rounded. The flesh from his cheekbones now hangs slack from his chin. He is bent forward to such a degree that he seems to suffer from a form of osteoporosis. He is left-handed and walks with a cane.[1]

His attendants bow before him and greet him as "awaited enlightened one."[2] This title has been bestowed upon him by believers throughout the Muslim world—both Sunnis and Shiites. He is more than a mighty warrior or a religious leader. To his followers, he is the rightly guided caliph—the *Mahdi*—who will appear during the last days of human history.[3]

His face now appears in stores, marketplaces, and humble dwellings throughout Islam. His name has become the favored name for baby boys in Saudi Arabia, Afghanistan, and Pakistan. Even the detainees at Guantanamo Bay bless his name and refer to him by his sacred title.[4]

His coming has been foretold by the Haddith, the collection of sacred teachings that supplement the Koran. In such writings, he is depicted as the prophet who will appear at a time when Muslims are oppressed throughout the world. He will unite the believers to fight off the vast army of their oppressors—the army of Yajuj wa-Majuj ("the infidel unbelievers"), led by the *Dabbah*, or "the Beast." He will lead the Muslims to victory and bring forth the Day of Islam, when all people throughout the world—believers and nonbelievers alike—will fall in total submission to the will of Allah.[5]

After restoring justice to the world by imposing *shariah* on all nations, he will lead the people in prayer at Mecca—an occasion at which Jesus will be present. Following the ceremony, he will rule over the Muslim people for seven years.[6]

The writings foretell that the long-awaited one will be a descendant of Muhammad through his daughter Fatima. He will have the same name as the Prophet, and his father will have the same name as the Prophet's father. He will have a distinctive forehead, a prominent nose, and a black mole on his face. He will be known for his generosity and altruism. He will arise from Arabia and will be called from a cave by Allah to serve as the savior of all true believers.[7]

The man in the village in Pakistan speaks of the president of the United States as *Dabbah*, the beast that he must slay, and of the American people as the Yajuj wa-Majuj, the nation of Gog that he must destroy.

In his edicts and official correspondence, he no longer signs his name as Osama bin Laden but as Osama bin Muhammad bin Laden.[8]

He is the "awaited enlightened one."

He is the mighty warrior of the Apocalypse.

He is the realization of nearly fourteen hundred years of Islamic history.

He is the *Mahdi*.

APPENDIXES

DECLARATION OF WAR AGAINST THE AMERICANS OCCUPYING THE LAND OF THE TWO HOLY PLACES

A Message from Osama bin Muhammad bin Laden unto His Muslim Brethren All Over the World Generally and in the Arab Peninsula Specifically

Praise be to Allah, we seek His help and ask for his pardon. We take refuge in Allah from our wrongs and bad deeds. Whoever has been guided by Allah will not be misled, and whoever has been misled, he will never be guided. I bear witness that there is no God except Allah, no associates with Him, and I bear witness that Muhammad is His slave and messenger.

"O you who believe! Be careful of your duty to Allah with the proper care which is due to Him, and do not die unless you are Muslim" (Aal Imraan 3:102); "O people be careful of your duty to your Lord, Who created you from a single being and created its mate of the same kind, and spread from these two, many men and women; and be careful of your duty to Allah, by whom you demand one of another your rights, and (be careful) to the ties of kinship; surely Allah ever watches over you" (An-Nisa 4:1); "O you who believe! Be careful of your duty to Allah and speak the right word; He will put your deeds into a right state for you, and forgive you your faults; and who ever obeys Allah and his Apostle, he indeed achieves a mighty success" (Al-Ahzaab 33:70–71).

Praise be to Allah, reporting the saying of the prophet Shu'aib: "I desire nothing but reform so far as I am able, and with none but Allah is the direction of my affair to the right and successful path; on him do I rely and to him do I turn" (Hu'd 11:88). Praise be to Allah, saying: "You are the best of the nations raised up for the benefit of men; you enjoin what is right and forbid the wrong and believe in Allah" (Aal Imraan 3:110).

Allah's blessing and salutations on His slave and messenger, who said: "The people are close to an all encompassing punishment from Allah if they see the oppressor and fail to restrain him."

It should not be hidden from you that the people of Islam had suffered from aggression, iniquity and injustice imposed on them by the Zionist/Crusaders alliance and their collaborators; to the extent that the Muslims' blood became the cheapest and their wealth as loot in the hands of the enemies. Their blood was spilled in Palestine and Iraq. The horrifying pictures of the massacre of Qana, in Lebanon, are still fresh in our memory. Massacres in Tajikistan, Burma, Kashmir, Assam, Philippine, Fatani, Ogadin, Somalia, Eritrea, Chechnya and in Bosnia-Herzegovina took place, massacres that send shivers in the body and shake the conscience. All of this and the world watched and heard, and not only didn't respond to these atrocities, but also with a clear conspiracy between the USA and its allies and under the cover of the iniquitous United Nations, the dispossessed people were even prevented from obtaining arms to defend themselves.

The people of Islam awakened and realized that they are the main target for the aggression of the Zionist/Crusaders alliance. All false claims and propaganda about "Human Rights" were hammered down and exposed by the massacres that took place against the Muslims in every part of the world. The latest and the greatest of these aggressions, incurred by the Muslims since the death of the Prophet (ALLAH'S BLESSING AND SALUTATIONS ON HIM) is the occupation of the land of the two Holy Places, the foundation of the house of Islam, the place of the revelation, the source of the message and the place of the noble Ka'ba, the Qiblah of all Muslims, by the armies of the American Crusaders and their allies. We bemoan this and can only say: "No power and power acquiring except through Allah."

Under the present circumstances, and under the banner of the blessed awakening which is sweeping the world in general and the Islamic world in particular, I meet with you today. And after a long absence, imposed on the scholars (Ulama) and callers (Da'ees) of Islam by the iniquitous crusaders movement under the leadership of the USA, who fears that they, the scholars and callers of Islam, will instigate the Ummah of Islam against its enemies as their ancestor scholars, may Allah be pleased with them like Ibn Taymiyyah and Al'iz Ibn Abdes Salaam did. And therefore the Zionist/Crusader alliance resorted to killing and arresting the truthful Ulama and the working Da'ees (We are not praising or sanctifying them; Allah sanctify whom He pleased). They killed the Mujahid Sheikh Abdullah Azzaam, and they arrested the Mujahid Sheikh Ahmad Yaseen and the Mujahid Sheikh Omar Abdur Rahman (in America).

By orders from the USA, they also arrested a large number of scholars, Da'ees and young people in the land of the two Holy Places, among them the prominent Sheikh Salman Al Oud'a and Sheikh Safar Al-Hawali and their brothers. We bemoan this and can only say: "No power and power acquiring except through Allah." We, my group and myself, have suffered some of this injustice ourselves; we have been prevented from addressing the Muslims. We have been pursued in Pakistan, Sudan and Afghanistan, hence this long absence on my part. But by the Grace of Allah, a safe base is now available in the high Hindukush Mountains in Khurasan; where the Grace of Allah destroyed the largest infidel military force of the world. And the myth of the superpower was withered in front of the Mujahadeen cries of Allahu Akbar (God is greater).

Today we work from the same mountains to lift the iniquity that had been imposed on the Ummah by the Zionist/Crusader alliance, particularly after they have occupied the blessed land around Jerusalem, route of the journey of the Prophet (ALLAH'S BLESSING AND SALUTATIONS ON HIM) and the land of the two Holy Places. We ask Allah to bestow us with victory, He is our Patron and He is the Most Capable. From here, today we begin the work, talking and discussing the ways of correcting what has happened to the Islamic world in general, and the Land of the two Holy Places in particular. We wish to study the means that we could follow to return the situation to its normal path, and to return to the people their own rights, particularly after the large damages and the great aggression on the life and the religion of the people. An injustice that had affected every section and group of the people: the civilians, military and security men, government officials and merchants, the young and the old people, as well as schools and university students. Hundred of thousands of the unemployed graduates, who became the widest section of the society, were also affected.

Injustice had affected the people of the industry and agriculture. It affected the people of the rural and urban areas. And almost everybody complains about something. The situation at the land of the two Holy Places became like a huge volcano at the verge of eruption that would destroy the Kufr and the corruption and its sources. The explosion at Riyadh and Al-Khobar is a warning of this volcanic eruption emerging as a result of the severe oppression, suffering, excessive iniquity, humiliation and poverty.

People are fully concerned about their everyday livings; everybody talks about the deterioration of the economy, inflation, ever-increasing debts, and jails full of prisoners. Government employees with limited income talk about debts of ten thousands and hundred thousands of Saudi Riyals. They complain that the value of the Riyal is greatly and continuously deteriorating among most of the main currencies. Great merchants and contractors speak about hundreds and thousands of millions of Riyals owed to them by the government. More than three hundred forty billion Riyals is owed by the government to the people in addition to the daily-accumulated interest, let alone the foreign debt. People wonder whether we are the largest oil exporting country! They even believe that this situation is a curse put on them by Allah for not objecting to the oppressive and illegitimate behavior and measures of the ruling regime: Ignoring the divine Shariah law; depriving people of their legitimate rights; allowing the American to occupy the land of the two Holy Places; imprisonment, unjustly, of the sincere scholars.

The honorable Ulamah and scholars as well as merchants, economists and eminent people of the country were all alerted by this disastrous situation. Quick efforts were made by each group to contain and to correct the situation. All agreed that the country is heading toward a great catastrophe, the depth of which is not known except by Allah. One big merchant commented: "The king is leading the state into 'sixty-six' folded disaster." We bemoan this and can only say: "No power and power acquiring except through Allah." Numerous princes share with the people their feelings, privately expressing their concerns and objecting to the corruption, repression, and the intimidation that is taking place in the country. But the competition between influential princes for personal gains and interest has destroyed the country. Through its course of actions, the regime has torn off its legitimacy:

(1) Suspension of the Islamic Shariah law and exchanging it with man-made civil law. The regime entered into a bloody confrontation with the truthful Ulamah and the righteous youths (we sanctify nobody; Allah sanctify Whom He pleaseth).

(2) The inability of the regime to protect the country, and allowing the enemy of the Ummah, the American Crusader forces, to

occupy the land for the longest of years. The Crusader forces became the main cause of our disastrous condition, particularly in the economical aspect of it, due to the unjustified heavy spending on these forces. As a result of the policy imposed on the country, especially in the field of oil industry, where production is restricted or expanded and prices are fixed to suit the American economy, ignoring the economy of the country. Expensive deals were imposed on the country to purchase arms. People are asking, what is the justification for the very existence of the regime then?

Quick efforts were made by individuals and by different groups of the society to contain the situation and to prevent the danger. They advised the government both privately and openly; they sent letters and poems, reports after reports, reminders after reminders, they explored every avenue and enlisted every influential man in their movement of reform and correction. They wrote with style of passion, diplomacy and wisdom asking for corrective measures and repentance from the "great wrongdoings and corruption" that had engulfed even the basic principles of the religion and the legitimate rights of the people.

But to our deepest regret the regime refused to listen to the people, accusing them of being ridiculous and imbecile. The matter got worse as previous wrongdoings were followed by misdeeds of greater magnitudes. All of this taking place in the land of the two Holy Places! It is no longer possible to be quiet. It is not acceptable to give a blind eye to this matter.

As the extent of these infringements reached the highest of levels and turned into demolishing forces threatening the very existence of the Islamic principles, a group of scholars who could take no more, supported by hundreds of retired officials, merchants, prominent and educated people, wrote to the King asking for implementation of the corrective measures. In 1411 AH (May 1991), at the time of the Gulf War, a letter, the famous letter of Shawwaal, with over four hundred signatures, was sent to the king demanding the lifting of oppression and the implementation of corrective actions. The king decided to humiliate those people and choose to ignore the content of their letter; and the very bad situation of the country became even worse. People, however, tried again and sent more letters and petitions. One particular report, the glorious Memorandum of Advice, was handed over to the king on Muharram, 1413 AH (July 1992), which tackled the problem, pointed out the illness and prescribed the medicine in an original, righteous and scientific style. It described the gaps and the shortcomings in the philosophy of the regime and suggested the required course of action and remedy. The report gave a description of:

(1) The intimidation and harassment suffered by the leaders of the society, the scholars, heads of tribes, merchants, academic teachers and other eminent individuals.
(2) The situation of the law within the country and the arbitrary declaration of what is Halal and Haram (lawful and unlawful) regardless of the Shariah as instituted by Allah.
(3) The state of the press and the media which became a tool of truth-hiding and misinformation; the media carried out the plan of the enemy of idolizing cult of certain personalities and spreading scandals among the believers to repel the people away from their religion, as Allah, the Exalted said: "Surely as for those who love that scandal should circulate between the believers, they shall have a grievous chastisement in this world and in the hereafter" (An-Noor 24:19).
(4) Abuse and confiscation of human rights.
(5) The financial and the economical situation of the country and the frightening future in the view of the enormous amount of debts and interest owed by the government; this is at the time when the wealth of the Ummah is being

wasted to satisfy personal desires of certain individuals—
while the government is imposing more custom duties and
taxes on the nation. (The prophet said about the woman
who committed adultery: "She repented in such a way sufficient to bring forgiveness to a custom collector!")

(6) The miserable situation of the social services and infrastructure, especially the water service and supply, the basic
requirement of life.

(7) The state of the ill-trained and poorly prepared army and
the impotence of its commander in chief, despite the
incredible amount of money that has been spent on the
army. The Gulf War clearly exposed the situation.

(8) Shariah law was suspended and man-made law was used
instead.

(9) And, as far as the foreign policy is concerned, the report
exposed not only how this policy has disregarded the Islamic
issues and ignored the Muslims, but also how help and support were provided to the enemy against the Muslims; the
cases of Gaza Ariha and the communist in the south of Yemen
are still fresh in the memory, and more can be said.

As stated by the people of knowledge, it is not a secret that to
use man-made law instead of the Shariah and to support the infidels
against the Muslims is one of the ten "voiders" that would strip a
person from his Islamic status (turn a Muslim into a Mushrik, non-
believer status). The All Mighty said: "And whoever did not judge
by what Allah revealed, those are the unbelievers" (Al-Maaidah
5:44), and, "But no! by your Lord! They do not believe (in reality)
until they make you a judge of that which has become a matter of
disagreement among them, and then do not find the slightest mis-
giving in their hearts as to what you have decided and submit with
entire submission" (An-Nissa 4:65).

In spite of the fact that the report was written with soft words and very diplomatic style, reminding of Allah, giving truthful sincere advice, and despite of the importance of advice in Islam being absolutely essential for those in charge of the people and the large number who signed this document as well as their supporters, all of that was not an intercession for the Memorandum. Its content was rejected and those who signed it and their sympathizers were ridiculed, prevented from travel, punished and even jailed. Therefore it is very clear that the advocates of correction and reform movement were very keen on using peaceful means in order to protect the unity of the country and to prevent bloodshed. Why is it then the regime closed all peaceful routes and pushed the people toward armed action, which remains the only choice left for them to implement righteousness and justice? To whose benefit do Prince Sultan and Prince Nayeff push the country into a civil war that will destroy everything? And why consult those who ignite internal feuds, playing the people against each other and instigate the policemen, the sons of the nation, to abort the reform movement, while leaving in peace and security such traitors who implement the policy of the enemy in order to bleed the financial and the human resources of the Ummah, and leaving the main enemy in the area—the American/Zionist alliance—to enjoy peace and security?! The advisor (Zaki Badr, the Egyptian ex-minister of the interior) to Prince Nayeff minister of interior was not acceptable even to his own country; he was sacked from his position there due to the filthy attitude and the aggression he exercised on his own people, yet he was warmly welcomed by Prince Nayeff to assist in sins and aggressions. He unjustly filled the prisons with the best sons of this Ummah and caused miseries to their mothers. Does the regime want to play the civilians against their military personnel and vice versa, like what had happened in some of the neighboring countries?!! No doubts this is the policy of the American/Israeli alliance as they are the first to benefit from this situation.

But with the grace of Allah, the majority of the nation, both civilians and military individuals, are aware of the wicked plan. They refused to be played against each other and to be used by the regime as a tool to carry out the policy of the American/Israeli alliance through their agent in our country: the Saudi regime. Therefore everyone agreed that the situation cannot be rectified (the shadow cannot be straightened when its source, the rod, is not straight either) unless the root of the problem is tackled. Hence it is essential to hit the main enemy who divided the Ummah into small and little countries and pushed it, for the last few decades, into a state of confusion. The Zionist/Crusader alliance moves quickly to contain and abort any "corrective movement" appearing in the Islamic countries. Different means and methods are used to achieve their target; on occasion the "movement" is dragged into an armed struggle at a predetermined unfavorable time and place. Sometime officials from the Ministry of Interior, who are also graduates of the colleges of the Shariah, are leashed out to mislead and confuse the nation and the Ummah (by wrong Fatwas) and to circulate false information about the movement. At other occasions some right-eous people were tricked into a war of words against the Ulama and the leaders of the movement, wasting the energy of the nation in discussing minor issues and ignoring the main one; that is, the uni-fication of the people under the divine law of Allah. In the shadow of these discussions and arguments, truthfulness is covered by the falsehood, and personal feuds and partisanship created among the people increasing the division and the weakness of the Ummah; priorities of the Islamic work are lost while the blasphemy and polytheism continue its grip and control over the Ummah. We should be alert to these atrocious plans carried out by the Ministry of Interior. The right answer is to follow what has been decided by the people of knowledge, as was said by Ibn Taymiyyah (Allah's mercy upon him): "People of Islam should join forces and support each other to get rid of the main 'Kufr' who is controlling the countries of the Islamic world, even to bear the lesser damage to get rid of the major one, that is, the great Kufr."

If there is more than one duty to be carried out, then the most important one should receive priority. Clearly after Belief (Imaan) there is no more important duty than pushing the American enemy out of the holy land. No other priority, except Belief, could be considered before it; the people of knowledge, as Ibn Taymiyyah said, stated: "To fight in defense of religion and Belief is a collective duty; there is no other duty after Belief than fighting the enemy who is corrupting the life and the religion. There are no preconditions for this duty and the enemy should be fought with one's best abilities (ref: Supplement of Fatawa). If it is not possible to push back the enemy except by the collective movement of the Muslim people, then there is a duty on the Muslims to ignore the minor differences among themselves; the ill effect of ignoring these differences, at a given period of time, is much less than the ill effect of the occupation of the Muslims' land by the main Kufr. Ibn Taymiyyah had explained this issue and emphasized the importance of dealing with the major threat at the expense of the minor one. He described the situation of the Muslims and the Mujahadeen and stated that even the military personnel who are not practicing Islam are not exempted from the duty of Jihad against the enemy.

Ibn Taymiyyah, after mentioning the Moguls (Tatar) and their behavior in changing the law of Allah, stated that "the ultimate aim of pleasing Allah, raising His word, instituting His religion and obeying His messenger (ALLAH'S BLESSING AND SALUTATIONS ON HIM) is to fight the enemy, in every aspect and in a complete manner; if the danger to the religion from not fighting is greater than that of fighting, then it is a duty to fight them even if the intention of some of the fighters is not pure, i.e., fighting for the sake of leadership (personal gain) or if they do not observe some of the rules and commandments of Islam. To repel the greater of the two dangers at the expense of the lesser one is an Islamic principle that should be observed. It was the tradition of the people of the Sunnah (Ahlul Sunnah) to join and fight with the righteous and nonrighteous men. Allah may support this religion by righteous and nonrighteous people as told by the prophet (ALLAH'S BLESSING AND SALUTATIONS ON HIM). If it is not possible to fight except with the help of nonrighteous military personnel and commanders, then there are two possibilities: either fighting will be ignored and the others, who are the great danger to this life and religion, will take control; or to fight with the help of nonrighteous rulers and therefore repel the greatest of the two dangers and implement most, though not all, of the Islamic laws. The latter option is the right duty to be carried out in these circumstances and in many other similar situations. In fact, many of the fights and conquests that took place after the time of Rashidoon, the guided Imams, were of this type" (Majmoo' al-Fatawa, 26/506). No one, not even a blind or a deaf person, can deny the presence of the widely spread mischiefs or the prevalence of the great sins that have reached the grievous iniquity of polytheism and to share with Allah in His sole right of sovereignty and making of the law. The All Mighty stated: "And when Luqman said to his son while he admonished him: O my son! Do not associate aught with Allah; most surely polytheism is a grievous iniquity" (Luqman 31:13). Man-fabricated laws were put forward permitting what has been forbidden by Allah such as usury (Riba) and other matters. Banks dealing in usury are competing, for lands, with the two Holy Places and declaring war against Allah by disobeying His order. "Allah has allowed trading and forbidden usury" (Baqarah 2:275). All of this is taking place at the vicinity of the Holy Mosque in the Holy Land! Allah (SWT) stated in His Holy Book a unique promise (that had not been promised to any other sinner) to the Muslims who deals in usury: "O you who believe! Be careful of your duty to Allah and relinquish what remains (due) from usury, if you are believers. But if you do (it) not, then be appraised of WAR from Allah and His Apostle" (Baqarah 2:278–79). This is for the "Muslim" who deals in usury (believing that it is a sin), what is it then for the person who makes himself a partner and equal to Allah by legalizing usury and other sins that have been forbidden by Allah? Despite of all of the above we see the government misled and dragging some of the righteous Ulamah and Da'ees away from the issue of objecting to the greatest of sins and Kufr. (We bemoan this and can only say: "No power and power acquiring except through Allah.")

Under such circumstances, to push the enemy, the greatest Kufr, out of the country is a prime duty. No other duty after Belief is more important than this duty. Utmost effort should be made to prepare and instigate the Ummah against the enemy, the American/Israeli alliance occupying the country of the two Holy Places and the route of the Apostle (Allah's Blessings and Salutations may be on him) to the Furthest Mosque (Al-Aqsa Mosque). Also to remind the Muslims not to be engaged in an internal war among themselves, as that will have grieve consequences, namely:

1. Consumption of the Muslims' human resources as most casualties and fatalities will be among the Muslim people.
2. Exhaustion of the economic and financial resources.
3. Destruction of the country's infrastructures.
4. Dissociation of the society.
5. Destruction of the oil industries. The presence of the USA Crusader military forces on land, sea and air of the states of the Islamic Gulf is the greatest danger threatening the largest oil reserve in the world. The existence of these forces in the area will provoke the people of the country and induce aggression on their religion, feelings and pride and push

them to take up armed struggle against the invaders occupying the land; therefore the spread of fighting in the region will expose the oil wealth to the danger of being burned up. The economic interest of the States of the Gulf and the land of the two Holy Places will be damaged and even a greater damage will be caused to the economy of the world. I would like here to alert my brothers, the Mujahadeen, the sons of the nation, to protect this (oil) wealth and not to include it in the battle as it is a great Islamic wealth and a large economic power essential for the soon-to-be established Islamic state, by Allah's Permission and Grace. We also warn the aggressors, the USA, against burning this Islamic wealth (a crime which they may commit in order to prevent it, at the end of the war, from falling in the hands of its legitimate owners and to cause economic damage to the competitors of the USA in Europe or the Far East, particularly Japan, which is the major consumer of the oil of the region).

6. Division of the land of the two Holy Places, and annexing of the northerly part of it by Israel. Dividing the land of the two Holy Places is an essential demand of the Zionist/Crusader alliance. The existence of such a large country with its huge resources under the leadership of the forthcoming Islamic State, by Allah's Grace, represents a serious danger to the very existence of the Zionist state in Palestine. The Nobel Ka'ba, the Qiblah of all Muslims, makes the land of the two Holy Places a symbol for the unity of the Islamic world. Moreover, the presence of the world's largest oil reserve makes the land of the two Holy Places an important economical power in the Islamic world. The sons of the two Holy Places are directly related to the lifestyle (Seerah) of their forefathers, the companions, May Allah be pleased with them. They consider the Seerah of their forefathers as a

source and an example for reestablishing the greatness of this Ummah and to raise the word of Allah again. Furthermore, the presence of a population of fighters in the south of Yemen, fighting in the cause of Allah, is a strategic threat to the Zionist/Crusader alliance in the area. The Prophet (ALLAH'S BLESSING AND SALUTATIONS ON HIM) said: "Around twelve thousand will emerge from Aden/Abian helping the cause of Allah and His messenger; they are the best, in the time between me and them." Narrated by Ahmad with a correct trustworthy reference.

7. An internal war is a great mistake, no matter what reasons there are for it. The presence of the occupier, the USA forces, will control the outcome of the battle for the benefit of the international Kufr.

I address now my brothers of the security and military forces and the national guards, may Allah preserve you for Islam and the Muslims people: O you protectors of unity and guardians of Faith. O you descendent of the ancestors who carried the light (torch) of guidance and spread it all over the world. O you grandsons of Sa'd Ibn Abi Waqqaas, Al-Mothanna Ibn Haritha Ash Shaybani, Al-Ga'ga' Ibn Amroo Al-Tameemi and those pious companions who fought Jihad alongside them; you competed to join the army and the guard forces with the intention to carry out Jihad in the cause of Allah raising His word and to defend the faith of Islam and the land of the two Holy Places against the invaders and the occupying forces. That is the ultimate level of believing in this religion "Deen." But the regime reversed these principles and their understanding, humiliating the Ummah and disobeying Allah. Half a century ago the rulers promised the Ummah to regain the first Qiblah, but fifty years later a new generation arrived and the promises have been changed; Al-Aqsa Mosque has been handed over to the Zion-

193

ists and the wounds of the Ummah are still bleeding there. At the time when the Ummah has not regained the first Qiblah and the route of the journey of the Prophet (Allah's Blessings and Salutations may be on him), and despite all of the above, the Saudi regime has stunted the Ummah in the remaining sanctities, the Holy city of Mecca and the mosque of the Prophet (Al-Masjid An-Nabawy), by calling the Christian army to defend the regime. The Crusaders were permitted to be in the land of the two Holy Places. Not surprisingly though, the King himself wore the cross on his chest. The country was widely opened from the north to the south and from east to the west for the Crusaders. The land was filled with the military bases of the USA and the allies. The regime became unable to keep control without the help of these bases. You know more than anybody else about the size, intention and the danger of the presence of the USA military bases in the area. The regime betrayed the Ummah and joined the Kufr, assisting and helping them against the Muslims. It is well known that this is one of the ten "voiders" of Islam, deeds of de-Islamization. By opening the Arab peninsula to the Crusaders, the regime disobeyed and acted against what has been enjoined by the messenger of Allah (Allah's Blessings and Salutations may be on him) while he was at the bed of his death: "Expel the polytheists out of the Arab Peninsula," narrated by Al-Bukhari; and: "If I survive, Allah willing, I'll expel the Jews and the Christians out of the Arab Peninsula," narrated by Saheeh Al-Jame' As Sagheer.

It is out of date and no longer acceptable to claim that the presence of the Crusaders is necessary and only a temporary measure to protect the land of the two Holy Places. Especially when the civil and the military infrastructures of Iraq were savagely destroyed, showing the depth of the Zionist/Crusaders hatred to the Muslims and their children and the rejection of the idea of replacing the Crusaders forces by an Islamic force composed of the sons of the country and other Muslim people. Moreover, the foundations of the claim and the claim itself were demolished and wiped out by the sequence of speeches given by the leaders of the Kuffar in America. The latest of these speeches was the one given by William Perry, the Defense Secretary, after the explosion in Al-Khobar, saying that the presence of the American soldiers there is to protect the interest of the USA. The imprisoned Sheikh Safar Al-Hawali, may Allah hasten his release, wrote a book of seventy pages; in it he presented evidence and proof that the presence of the Americans in the Arab Peninsula is a preplanned military occupation. The regime wants to deceive the Muslim people in the same manner as when the Palestinian fighters, Mujahadeen, were deceived, causing the loss of Al-Aqsa Mosque. In 1304 AH (1936 CE) the awakened Muslim nation of Palestine started their great struggle, Jihad, against the British occupying forces. Britain was impotent to stop the Mujahadeen and their Jihad, but their devil inspired that there is no way to stop the armed struggle in Palestine unless through their agent King Abdul Azeez, who managed to deceive the Mujahadeen. King Abdul Azeez carried out his duty to his British masters. He sent his two sons to meet the Mujahadeen leaders and to inform them that King Abdul Azeez would guarantee the promises made by the British government, of leaving the area and responding positively to the demands of the Mujahadeen if the latter stopped their Jihad. And so King Abdul Azeez caused the loss of the first Qiblah of the Muslim people. The King joined the Crusaders against the Muslims and instead of supporting the Mujahadeen in the cause of Allah, to liberate the Al-Aqsa Mosque, he disappointed and humiliated them.

Today, his son, King Fahd, is trying to deceive the Muslims for the second time so as to lose what is left of the sanctities. When the Islamic world resented the arrival of the Crusader forces to the land of the two Holy Places, the king told lies to the Ulamah (who issued Fatwas about the arrival of the Americans) and to the gathering of the Islamic leaders at the conference of Rabitah, which was held in the Holy City of Mecca. The King said: "The issue is simple, the American and the alliance forces will leave the area in few months." Today it is seven years since their arrival and the regime is not able to move them out of the country. The regime has made no confession about its inability and carries on lying to the people, claiming that the Americans will leave. But never, never again! A believer will not be bitten twice from the same hole or snake! Happy is the one who takes note of the sad experience of others!! Instead of motivating the army, the guards and the security men to oppose the occupiers, the regime used these men to protect the invaders and further deepened the humiliation and the betrayal. (We bemoan this and can only say: "No power and power acquiring except through Allah.") To that little group of men within the army, police and security forces who have been tricked and pressured by the regime to attack the Muslims and spill their blood, we would like to remind them of the narration: "I promise war against those who take my friends as their enemy," narrated by Al-Bukhari. Al-Bukhari (Allah's Blessings and Salutations may be on him) also narrated: "In the day of judgment a man comes holding another and complains of being slain by him. Allah, blessed be His Names, asks: 'Why did you slay him?' The accused replies: 'I did so that all exaltation may be yours.' Allah, blessed be His Names, says: 'All exaltation is indeed mine!' Another man comes holding a fourth with a similar complaint. Allah, blessed be His Names, asks: 'Why did you kill him?' The accused replies: 'I did so that exaltation may be for Mr. X!' Allah, blessed be His Names, says: 'Exaltation is mine, not for Mr. X! Carry all the slain man's sins and proceed to the Hell fire!" In another wording of An-Nasa'i: "The accused says: 'for strengthening the rule or kingdom of Mr. X.'"

Today your brothers and sons, the sons of the two Holy Places, have started their Jihad in the cause of Allah, to expel the occupying enemy out of the country of the two Holy places. And there is no doubt you would like to carry out this mission too, in order to reestablish the greatness of this Ummah and to liberate its occupied sanctities. Nevertheless, it must be obvious to you that, due to the imbalance of power between our armed forces and the enemy forces, a suitable means of fighting must be adopted, i.e., using fast-moving light forces that work under complete secrecy. In other words, to initiate a guerrilla warfare so that the sons of the nation, rather than the military forces, will take part in it. And, as you know, it is wise, in the present circumstances, for the armed military forces not to be engaged in conventional fighting with the forces of the Crusader enemy (the exceptions are the bold and the forceful operations carried out by the members of the armed forces individually, that is, without the movement of the formal forces in its conventional shape and hence the responses will not be directed, strongly, against the army) unless a big advantage is likely to be achieved; and great losses induced on the enemy side (that would shake and destroy its foundations and infrastructures) that will help to expel the enemy defeated out of the country. The Mujahadeen, your brothers and sons, request that you support them in every possible way by supplying them with the necessary information, materials and arms. Security men are especially asked to cover up for the Mujahadeen and to assist them as much as possible against the occupying enemy; and to spread rumors, fear and discouragement among the members of the enemy forces. We bring to your attention that the regime, in order to create a friction and feud between the Mujahadeen and yourselves, might resort to taking deliberate action against personnel of the security, guards and military forces and blame the Mujahadeen for these actions. The regime should not be allowed to have such an opportunity. The regime is fully responsible for what has been incurred by the country and the nation; however, the occupying American enemy is the principle and the main cause of the situation. Therefore, efforts should be concentrated on destroying, fighting and killing the enemy until, by the Grace of Allah, it is completely defeated. The time will come by the permission of Allah when you'll perform your decisive role so that the word of Allah will be supreme and the word of the infidels (Kaferoon) will be the inferior. You will hit with an iron fist against the aggressors. You'll reestablish the normal course and give the people their rights and carry out your true Islamic duty. Allah willing, I'll have a separate talk about these issues.

My Muslim Brothers (particularly those of the Arab Peninsula):

The money you pay to buy American goods will be transformed into bullets and used against our brothers in Palestine and tomorrow (future) against our sons in the land of the two Holy Places. By buying these goods we are strengthening their economy while our dispossession and poverty increases.

Muslims Brothers of land of the two Holy Places:

It is incredible that our country is the world's largest buyer of arms from the USA and the area's biggest commercial partner of the Americans who are assisting their Zionist brothers in occupying Palestine and in evicting and killing the Muslims there, by providing arms, men and financial support. To deny these occupiers the enormous revenues of their trading with our country is a very important help for our Jihad against them. To express our anger and hate to them is a very important moral gesture. By doing so we would have taken part in (the process of) cleansing our sanctities from the Crusaders and the Zionists and forcing them, by the Permission of Allah, to leave disappointed and defeated.

We expect the women of the land of the two Holy Places and other countries to carry out their role in boycotting the American goods. If economic boycotting is intertwined with the military operations of the Mujahadeen, then defeating the enemy will be even nearer, by the Permission of Allah. However, if Muslims don't cooperate and support their Mujahadeen brothers, then, in effect, they are supplying the army of the enemy with financial help and extending the war and increasing the suffering of the Muslims.

The security and the intelligence services of the entire world cannot force a single citizen to buy the goods of his/her enemy. Economic boycotting of American goods is a very effective weapon for hitting and weakening the enemy, and it is not under the control of the security forces of the regime. Before closing my talk, I have a very important message to the youth of Islam, men of the brilliant future of the Ummah of Muhammad (ALLAH'S BLESSING AND SALUTATIONS ON HIM). We talk with the youth about their duty in this difficult period in the history of our Ummah—a period in which the youth and no one else came forward to carry out the various and different duties. While some of the well-known individuals hesitated in their duty of defending Islam and saving themselves and their wealth from the injustice, aggression and terror exercised by the government, the youth (may Allah protect them) were forthcoming and raised the banner of Jihad against the American/Zionist alliance occupying the sanctities of Islam. Others who have been tricked into loving this materialistic world, and those who have been terrorized by the government, choose to give legitimacy to the greatest betrayal, the occupation of the land of the two Holy Places (We bemoan this and can only say: "No power and power acquiring except through Allah"). We are not surprised at the actions of our youth. The youth were the companions of Muhammad (Allah's Blessings and Salutations may be on him). Was it not the youths themselves who killed Aba Jahl, the Pharaoh of this Ummah? Our youths are the best descendents of the best ancestors.

Abdul Rahman Ibn Awf (may Allah be pleased with him) said: "I was at Badr where I noticed two youths, one to my right and the other to my left. One of them asked me quietly (so not to be heard by the other): 'O uncle point out Aba Jahl to me.' 'What do you want him for?' said Abdul Rahman. The boy answered: 'I have been informed that he, Aba Jahl, abused the Messenger of Allah. I swear by Allah, who has my soul in His hand, that if I see Aba Jahl, I'll not let my shadow depart his shadow till one of us is dead.'" "I was astonished," said Abdul Rahman. "Then the other youth said the same thing as the first one. Subsequently, I saw Aba Jahl among the people; I said to the boys, 'Do you see? This is the man you are asking me about.' The two youths hit Aba Jahl with their swords till he was dead." Allah is the greatest, Praise be to Him: Two youths of young age but with great perseverance, enthusiasm, courage and pride for the religion of Allah, each one of them asking about the most important act of killing that should be imposed on the enemy. That is the killing of the pharaoh of this Ummah Aba Jahl, the leader of the unbelievers (Mushrikeen) at the battle of Badr. The role of Abdul Rahman Ibn Awf, may Allah be pleased with him, was to direct the two youths toward Aba Jahl. That was the perseverance and the enthusiasm of the youth of that time, and that was the perseverance and the enthusiasm of their fathers. It is this role that is now required from the people who have the expertise and knowledge in fighting the enemy. They should guide their brothers and sons in this matter; once that has been done, then our youth will repeat what their forefathers had said before: "I swear by Allah if I see him I'll not let my shadow depart from his shadow till one of us is dead."

And the story of Abdur Rahman Ibn Awf about Ummayyah Ibn Khalaf shows the extent of Bilal's (may Allah be pleased with him) persistence in killing the head of the Kufr: "The head of Kufr is Ummayyah Ibn Khalaf. . . . I shall live not if he survives," said Bilal.

A few days ago the news agencies reported that the Defense Secretary of the Crusading Americans had said that "the explosions at Riyadh and Al-Khobar had taught him one lesson: that is, not to withdraw when attacked by coward terrorists."

We say to the Defense Secretary that his talk can induce a grieving mother to laughter and shows the fears that have enshrined you all. Where was this false courage of yours when the explosion in Beirut took place on 1983 CE (1403 AH)? You were turned into scattered pits and pieces at that time; 241 mainly Marine soldiers were killed. And where was this courage of yours when two explosions made you leave Aden in less than twenty-four hours?

But your most disgraceful case was in Somalia; where, after vigorous propaganda about the power of the USA and its post–Cold War leadership of the New World Order, you moved tens of thousands of international forces, including twenty-eight thousand American soldiers into Somalia. However, when a few of your soldiers were killed in minor battles and one American pilot was dragged in the streets of Mogadishu, you left the area carrying disappointment, humiliation, defeat and your dead with you. Clinton appeared in front of the whole world threatening and promising revenge, but these threats were merely a preparation for withdrawal. You were disgraced by Allah and you withdrew; the extent of your impotence and weaknesses became very clear. It was a pleasure for the "heart" of every Muslim and a remedy to the "chests" of believing nations to see you defeated in the three Islamic cities of Beirut, Aden and Mogadishu.

I say to the Secretary of Defense: The sons of the land of the two Holy Places came out to fight against the Russian in Afghanistan, the Serb in Bosnia-Herzegovina and today they are fighting in Chechnya and, by the Permission of Allah, they have been made victorious over your partner, the Russians. By the command of Allah, they are also fighting in Tajikistan. I say: Since the sons of the land of the two Holy Places feel and strongly believe that fighting (Jihad) against the Kuffar in every part of the world is absolutely essential, then they would be even more enthusiastic, more powerful and larger in number when fighting on their own land, the place of their births, defending the greatest of their sanctities, the noble Ka'ba (the Qiblah of all Muslims). They know that the Muslims of the world will assist and help them to victory. To liberate their sanctities is the greatest of issues concerning all Muslims; it is the duty of every Muslim in this world. I say to you William (Defense Secretary), that these youths love death as you love life. They inherit dignity, pride, courage, generosity, truthfulness and sacrifice from father to father. They are most delivering and steadfast at war. They inherit these values from their ancestors (even from the time of the Jaheliyyah, before Islam). These values were approved and completed by the arrival of Islam as stated by the messenger of Allah (Allah's Blessings and Salutations may be on him): "I have been sent to perfect the good values" (Saheeh Al-Jame' As Sagheer). When the pagan King Amroo Ibn Hind tried to humiliate the pagan Amroo Ibn Kulthoom, the latter cut off the head of the king with his sword, rejecting aggression, humiliation and indignation.

If the king oppresses the people excessively, we refuse to submit to humiliation. By which legitimacy (or command), O Amroo bin Hind, do you want us to be degraded? By which legitimacy (or command), O Amroo bin Hind, do you listen to our foes and disrespect us? Our toughness, O Amroo, has tired the enemies before you, never giving in! Our youths believe in paradise after death. They believe that taking part in fighting will not bring their day nearer; and staying behind will not postpone their day either. Exalted be to Allah who said: "And a soul will not die but with the permission of Allah, the term is fixed" (Aal Imraan 3:145). Our youths believe in the saying of the messenger of Allah (Allah's Blessings and Salutations may be on him): "O boy, I teach a few words; guard (guard the cause of, keep the commandments of)

Allah, then He guards you, guard (the cause of) Allah, then He will
be with you; if you ask (for your need), ask Allah, if you seek assistance, seek Allah's; and know definitely that if the Whole World
gathered to (bestow) profit on you they will not profit you except
with what was determined for you by Allah, and if they gathered to
harm you they will not harm you except with what has been determined for you by Allah; Pen lifted, papers dried, it is fixed, nothing
in these truths can be changed" (Saheeh Al-Jame' As Sagheer).

Our youth took note of the meaning of the poetic verse:

If death is a predetermined must, then it is a shame to die cowardly.

And the other poet saying:

Who do not die by the sword will die by other reason; many
causes are there but one death.

These youths believe in what has been told by Allah and His
messenger (Allah's Blessings and Salutations may be on him) about
the greatness of the reward for the Mujahadeen and Martyrs; Allah,
the most exalted said: "And so for those who are slain in the way of
Allah, He will by no means allow their deeds to perish. He will
guide them and improve their condition and cause them to enter the
garden paradise that He has made known to them" (Muhammad
47:46). Allah the Exalted also said: "Do not speak of those who are
slain in Allah's way as dead; nay, they are alive, but you do not per-
ceive" (Baqarah 2:154). His messenger (Allah's Blessings and
Salutations may be on him) said: "For those who strive in His
cause, Allah prepared a hundred degrees (levels) in paradise; the
distance between two degrees is as the distance between heaven and
earth" (Saheeh Al-Jame' As Sagheer). He (Allah's Blessings and
Salutations may be on him) also said: "The best of the martyrs are
those who do NOT turn their faces away from the battle till they are

203

killed. They are in the high level of Jannah (paradise). Their Lord laughs to them (in pleasure), and when your Lord laughs to a slave of His, He will not hold him to an account," narrated by Ahmad with correct and trustworthy reference. And: "A martyr will not feel the pain of death except like how you feel when you are pinched" (Saheeh Al-Jame' As Sagheer). This teacher also said: "A martyr's privileges are guaranteed by Allah; forgiveness with the first gush of his blood, he will be shown his seat in paradise, he will be decorated with the jewels of belief (Imaan), married off to the beautiful ones, protected from the test in the grave, assured security in the day of judgment, crowned with the crown of dignity, a ruby of which is better than this whole world (Duniah) and its entire content, wedded to seventy-two of the pure Houries (beautiful ones of Paradise) and his intercession on the behalf of seventy of his relatives will be accepted," narrated by Ahmad and At-Tirmithi (with the correct and trustworthy reference).

Those youths know that their reward in fighting you, the USA, is double their reward in fighting someone else not from the people of the book. They have no intention except to enter paradise by killing you. An infidel, an enemy of God, like you cannot be in the same hell with his righteous executioner. Our youths chant and recite the word of Allah, the most exalted:

"Fight them; Allah will punish them by your hands and bring them to disgrace, and assist you against them and heal the heart of a believing people" (Al-Taubah 9:14) and the words of the Prophet (ALLAH'S BLESSING AND SALUTATIONS ON HIM): "I swear by Him, who has my soul in His hand, that no man killed fighting them today, patiently attacking and not retreating, surely Allah will let him into paradise." And his (Allah's Blessings and Salutations may be on him) saying to them: "Get up to a paradise as wide as heaven and earth."

The youths also recite the All Mighty words: "So when you

meet in battle those who disbelieve, then smite the necks..."
(Muhammad 47:19).

Those youths will not ask you (William Perry) for explanations.
They will tell you, singing, there is nothing between us that needs
to be explained, there is only killing and neck smiting.

And they will say to you what their grandfather, Haroon Ar
Rasheed, Ameer ul-Mu'meneen, replied to your grandfather, Nagfoor, the Byzantine emperor, when he threatened the Muslims:
"From Haroon Ar Rasheed, Ameer ul-Mu'meneen, to Nagfoor, the
dog of the Romans; the answer is what you will see, not what you
hear." Haroon El Rasheed led the armies of Islam to battle and
handed Nagfoor a devastating defeat.

The youths you called cowards are competing among themselves for fighting and killing you, reciting what one of them said:

"The Crusader army became dust when we detonated Al-
Khobar with courageous youth of Islam fearing no danger."

If (they are) threatened: The tyrants will kill you; they reply,
"My death is a victory. I did not betray that king, and he did betray
our Qiblah! And he permitted in the holy country the most filthy
sort of humans. I have made an oath by Allah, the Great, to fight
whoever rejected the faith.

For more than a decade, they carried arms on their shoulders in
Afghanistan, and they have made vows to Allah that as long as they
are alive, they will continue to carry arms against you until you are,
Allah willing, expelled, defeated and humiliated. They will carry
on as long as they live, saying:

O William, tomorrow you will know which young man is confronting your misguided brethren!

A youth fighting in smiles, returning with the spear colored
red.

May Allah keep me close to knights, humans in peace,
demons in war.

Lions in Jungle but their teeth are spears and Indian swords.

The horses witness that I push them hard forward in the fire of battle.

The dust of the battle bears witnesses for me, so also the fighting itself, the pens and the books!

So to abuse the grandsons of the companions, may Allah be pleased with them, by calling them cowards and challenging them by refusing to leave the land of the two Holy Places shows the insanity and the imbalance you are suffering from. Its appropriate remedy, however, is in the hands of the youths of Islam, as the poet said:

I am willing to sacrifice self and wealth for knights who never disappointed me, Knights who are never fed up or deterred by death, even if the mill of war turns.

In the heat of battle they do not care, and cure the insanity of the enemy by their "insane" courage.

Terrorizing you, while you are carrying arms on our land, is a legitimate and morally demanded duty. It is a legitimate right well known to all humans and other creatures. Your example and our example are like that of a snake that entered into a house of a man and got killed by him. The coward is the one who lets you walk, while carrying arms, freely on his land and provides you with peace and security.

Those youths are different from your soldiers. Your problem will be how to convince your troops to fight, while our problem will be how to restrain our youths to wait for their turn in fighting and in operations. These youths are commendable and praiseworthy.

They stood up tall to defend the religion at the time when the government misled the prominent scholars and tricked them into issuing Fatwas (that have no basis neither in the book of Allah, nor in the Sunnah of His prophet [Allah's Blessings and Salutations may be on him]) of opening the land of the two Holy Places for the Christians armies and handing the Al-Aqsa Mosque to the Zionists.

Twisting the meanings of the holy text will not change this fact at all. They deserve the praise of the poet:

I rejected all the critics, who chose the wrong way.
   I rejected those who enjoy fireplaces in clubs discussing eternally.
   I rejected those, who in spite being lost, think they are at the goal.
   I respect those who carried on not asking or bothering about the difficulties.
   Never letting up from their goals, in spite all hardships of the road.
   Whose blood is the oil for the flame guiding in the darkness of confusion.
   I feel still the pain of (the loss) Al-Quds in my internal organs.
   That loss is like a burning fire in my intestines.
   I did not betray my covenant with God, when even states did betray it!

As their grandfather Assim bin Thabit said, rejecting a surrender offer of the pagans:

What for an excuse I had to surrender, while I am still able, having arrows and my bow having a tough string?
   Death is truth and ultimate destiny, and life will end anyway.
   If I do not fight you, then my mother must be insane!

The youths hold you responsible for all of the killings and evictions of the Muslims and the violation of the sanctities, carried out by your Zionist brothers in Lebanon; you openly supplied them with arms and finance. More than 600,000 Iraqi children have died due to lack of food and medicine and as a result of the unjustifiable aggression (sanctions) imposed on Iraq and its nation.

The children of Iraq are our children. You, the USA, together with the Saudi regime, are responsible for the shedding of the blood of these innocent children. Due to all of that, whatever treaty you have with our country is now null and void.

The treaty of Hudaybiyyah was cancelled by the messenger of Allah (Allah's Blessings and Salutations may be on him), once Quraysh had assisted Bani Bakr against Khusa'ah, the allies of the prophet (Allah's Blessings and Salutations may be on him). The prophet (Allah's Blessings and Salutations may be on him) fought Quraysh and conquered Mecca. He (Allah's Blessings and Salutations may be on him) considered the treaty with Bani Qainuqa' void because one of their Jews publicly hurt one Muslim woman, one single woman, at the market. Let alone then, the killing you caused to hundreds of thousands Muslims and occupying their sanctities. It is now clear that those who claim that the blood of the American soldiers (the enemy occupying the land of the Muslims) should be protected are merely repeating what is imposed on them by the regime, fearing aggression and interested in saving themselves. It is a duty now on every tribe in the Arab Peninsula to fight, Jihad, in the cause of Allah and to cleanse the land from those occupiers. Allah knows that their blood is permitted (to be spilled) and their wealth is a booty; their wealth is a booty to those who kill them. The most Exalted said in the verse of As Sayef, the Sword: "So when the sacred months have passed away, then slay the idolaters wherever you find them, and take them captive and besiege them and lie in wait for them in every ambush" (Al-Taubah 9:5). Our youths know that the humiliation suffered by the Muslims as a result of the occupation of their sanctities cannot be kicked out and removed except by explosions and Jihad. As the poet said:

The walls of oppression and humiliation cannot be demolished except in a rain of bullets. The freeman does not surrender leadership to infidels and sinners.

Without shedding blood no degradation and branding can be removed from the forehead.

I remind the youth of the Islamic world, who fought in Afghanistan and Bosnia-Herzegovina with their wealth, pens, tongues and themselves, that the battle has not finished yet. I remind them about the talk between Jibreel (Gabriel) and the messenger of Allah (Allah's Blessings and Salutations may be on both of them) after the battle of Ahzab when the messenger of Allah (Allah's Blessings and Salutations may be on him) returned to Medina and before putting his sword aside, when Jibreel (Allah's Blessings and Salutations may be on him) descended, saying: "Are you putting your sword aside? By Allah, the angels haven't dropped their arms yet; march with your companions to Bani Quraydah, I am (going) ahead of you to throw fear in their hearts and to shake their fortresses on them." Jibreel marched with the angels (Allah's Blessings and Salutations may be on them all), followed by the messenger of Allah (Allah's Blessings and Salutations may be on him) marching with the immigrants (Muhajeroon) and supporters (Ansar) (narrated by Al-Burkhari).

These youths know that if one is not to be killed, one will die (anyway), and the most honorable death is to be killed in the way of Allah. They are even more determined after the martyrdom of the four heroes who bombed the Americans in Riyadh. Those youths who raised high the head of the Ummah and humiliated the Americans, the occupier, by their operation in Riyadh. They remember the poetry of Ja'far, the second commander in the battle of Mu'tah, in which three thousand Muslims faced over a hundred thousand Romans:

How good is the Paradise and its nearness, good with cool drink.
    But the Romans are promised punishment (in Hell), if I meet
them.
    I will fight them.

And the poetry of Abdullah bin Rawaha, the third commander
in the battle of Mu'tah, after the martyrdom of Ja'far, when he felt
some hesitation:

O my soul if you do not get killed, you are going to die, anyway.
    This is death pool in front of you!

You are getting what you have wished for (martyrdom) before,
and you follow the example of the two previous commanders, you
are rightly guided!

    As for our daughters, wives, sisters and mothers, they should
take prime example from the prophet's (Allah's Blessings and Salutations may be on him) pious female companions, may Allah be
pleased with them; they should adopt the lifestyle (Seerah) of the
female companions of courage, sacrifice and generosity in the cause
of the supremacy of Allah's religion. They should remember the
courage and the personality of Fatima, daughter of Khatab, when
she accepted Islam and stood up in front of her brother, Omar Ibn
Al-Khatab and challenged him (before he became a Muslim) saying:
"O Omar, what will you do if the truth is not in your religion?!" And
to remember the stand of Asma', daughter of Abu Bakr, on the day
of Hijra, when she attended the Messenger and his companion in the
cave and split her belt in two pieces for them. And to remember the
stand of Naseeba Bent Ka'b, striving to defend the messenger of
Allah (Allah's Blessings and Salutations may be on him) on the day
of Uhud, in which she suffered twelve injuries, one of which was so
deep it left a deep, lifelong scar! They should remember the generosity of the early women of Islam who raised finances for the

Muslim army by selling their jewelry. Our women set a tremendous example of generosity in the cause of Allah; they motivated and encouraged their sons, brothers and husbands to fight in the cause of Allah in Afghanistan, Bosnia-Herzegovina, Chechnya, and in other countries. We ask Allah to accept from them these deeds, and may He help their fathers, brothers, husbands and sons. May Allah strengthen the belief (Imaan) of our women in the way of generosity and sacrifice for the supremacy of the word of Allah. Our women weep not, except over men who fight in the cause of Allah; our women instigate their brothers to fight in the cause of Allah.

Our women bemoan only fighters in the cause of Allah, as said:
Do not moan on any one except a lion in the woods, courageous in the burning wars.
Let me die dignified in wars, honorable death is better than my current life.

Our women encourage to Jihad saying:

Prepare yourself like a struggler, the matter is bigger than words!
Are you going to leave us else for the wolves of Kufr eating our wings?!
The wolves of Kufr are mobilizing all evil persons from everywhere!
Where are the freemen defending free women by the arms?
Death is better than life in humiliation! Some scandals and shames will never be otherwise eradicated.

My Muslim Brothers of the World:
Your brothers in Palestine and in the land of the two Holy Places are calling upon your help and asking you to take part in fighting against the enemy, your enemy and their enemy, the Americans and the Israelis. They are asking you to do whatever you can,

with one's own means and ability, to expel the enemy, humiliated and defeated, out of the sanctities of Islam. Exalted be Allah, who said in His book: "And if they ask your support, because they are oppressed in their faith, then support them!" (Al-Anfaal 8:72).

O you horses (soldiers) of Allah, ride and march on. This is the time of hardship, so be tough. And know that your gathering and cooperation in order to liberate the sanctities of Islam is the right step toward unifying the word of the Ummah under the banner of "No God but Allah."

From our place we raise our palms humbly to Allah asking Him to bestow on us His guide in every aspect of this issue.

Our Lord, we ask you to secure the release of the truthful scholars (Ulama) of Islam and pious youths of the Ummah from their imprisonment. O Allah, strengthen them and help their families.

Our Lord, the people of the cross have come with their horses (soldiers) and occupied the land of the two Holy Places. And the Zionist Jews fiddling as they wish with the Al-Aqsa Mosque, the route of the ascendance of the messenger of Allah (ALLAH'S BLESSING AND SALUTATIONS ON HIM). Our Lord, shatter their gathering, divide them among themselves, shake the earth under their feet and give us control over them; Our Lord, we take refuge in you from their deeds and take you as a shield between us and them.

Our Lord, show us a black day for them!

Our Lord, show us the wonderment of your ability in them!

Our Lord, You are the Revealer of the book, Director of the clouds, You defeated the allies (Ahzab); defeat them and make us victorious over them.

Our Lord, You are the one who helps us and You are the one who assists us, with Your Power we move and by Your Power we fight. On You we rely and You are our cause. Our Lord, those youths got together to make Your religion victorious and raise Your banner. Our Lord, send them Your help and strengthen their hearts.

Our Lord, make the youth of Islam steadfast and descend patience on them and guide their shots!

Our Lord, unify the Muslims and bestow love among their hearts!

Our Lord, pour down upon us patience, make our steps firm, and assist us against the unbelieving people!

Our Lord, do not lay on us a burden as Thou didst lay on those before us; Our Lord, do not impose upon us that which we have no strength to bear; and pardon us and grant us protection and have mercy on us, Thou art our patron, so help us against the unbelieving people.

Our Lord, guide this Ummah, and make the right conditions (by which) the people of your obedience will be in dignity and the people of disobedience in humiliation, and by which the good deeds are enjoined and the bad deeds are forbidden.

Our Lord, bless Muhammad, Your slave and messenger, his family and descendants, and companions and salute him with a (becoming) salutation.

And our last supplication is: All praise is due to Allah.

Osama bin Muhammad bin Laden

Friday, August 23, 1996

Hindukush Mountains, Khurasan, Afghanistan.

JIHAD AGAINST
JEWS AND CRUSADERS

World Islamic Statement
February 23, 1998

*Statement signed by Sheikh Osama bin-Muhammad bin Laden;
Ayman al-Zawahiri, leader of the Jihad Group in Egypt; Abu-
Yasir Rifa'i Ahmad Taha, a leader of the Islamic Group; Sheikh
Mir Hamzah, secretary of the Jamiat-ul-Ulema-e-Pakistan; and
Fazlul Rahman, leader of the Jihad Movement in Bangladesh.*

Praise be to Allah, who revealed the Book, controls the clouds, defeats factionalism, and says in His Book: "But when the forbidden months are past, then fight and slay the pagans wherever ye find them, seize them, beleaguer them, and lie in wait for them in every stratagem (of war)"; and peace be upon our Prophet, Muhammad bin-'Abdallah, who said: "I have been sent with the sword between my hands to ensure that no one but Allah is worshipped, Allah who put my livelihood under the shadow of my spear and who inflicts humiliation and scorn on those who disobey my orders." The Arabian Peninsula has never—since Allah made it flat, created its desert, and encircled it with seas—been stormed by any forces like the Crusader armies now spreading in it like locusts, consuming its riches and destroying its plantations. All

215

this is happening at a time when nations are attacking Muslims like people fighting over a plate of food. In the light of the grave situation and the lack of support, we and you are obliged to discuss current events, and we should all agree on how to settle the matter.

No one argues today about three facts that are known to everyone; we will list them, in order to remind everyone:

First, for over seven years the United States has been occupying the lands of Islam in the holiest of places, the Arabian Peninsula, plundering its riches, dictating to its rulers, humiliating its people, terrorizing its neighbors, and turning its bases in the Peninsula into a spearhead through which to fight the neighboring Muslim peoples.

If some people have formerly debated the fact of the occupation, all the people of the Peninsula have now acknowledged it. The best proof of this is the Americans' continuing aggression against the Iraqi people using the Peninsula as a staging post, even though all its rulers are against their territories being used to that end, still they are helpless.

Second, despite the great devastation inflicted on the Iraqi people by the Crusader-Zionist alliance, and despite the huge number of those killed, in excess of 1 million . . . despite all this, the Americans are once again trying to repeat the horrific massacres, as though they are not content with the protracted blockade imposed after the ferocious war or the fragmentation and devastation.

So now they come to annihilate what is left of this people and to humiliate their Muslim neighbors.

Third, if the Americans' aims behind these wars are religious and economic, the aim is also to serve the Jews' petty state and divert attention from its occupation of Jerusalem and murder of Muslims there. The best proof of this is their eagerness to destroy Iraq, the strongest neighboring Arab state, and their endeavor to fragment all the states of the region such as Iraq, Saudi Arabia,

Egypt, and Sudan into paper statelets and through their disunion and weakness to guarantee Israel's survival and the continuation of the brutal Crusade occupation of the Peninsula.

All these crimes and sins committed by the Americans are a clear declaration of war on Allah, his messenger, and Muslims. And ulema have throughout Islamic history unanimously agreed that the jihad is an individual duty if the enemy destroys the Muslim countries. This was revealed by Imam bin-Qadamah in "Al-Mughni," Imam al-Kisa'i in "Al-Bada'i," al-Qurtubi in his interpretation, and the shaykh of al-Islam in his books, where he said: "As for the militant struggle, it is aimed at defending sanctity and religion, and it is a duty as agreed. Nothing is more sacred than belief except repulsing an enemy who is attacking religion and life."

On that basis, and in compliance with Allah's order, we issue the following fatwa to all Muslims.

The ruling to kill the Americans and their allies—civilians and military—is an individual duty for every Muslim who can do it in any country in which it is possible to do it, in order to liberate the Al-Aqsa Mosque and the holy mosque in Mecca from their grip, and in order for their armies to move out of all the lands of Islam, defeated and unable to threaten any Muslim. This is in accordance with the words of Almighty Allah, "and fight the pagans all together as they fight you all together," and "fight them until there is no more tumult or oppression, and there prevail justice and faith in Allah."

This is in addition to the words of Almighty Allah: "And why should ye not fight in the cause of Allah and of those who, being weak, are ill-treated and oppressed—women and children, whose cry is 'Our Lord, rescue us from this town, whose people are oppressors; and raise for us from thee one who will help!'"

We—with Allah's help—call on every Muslim who believes in

Allah and wishes to be rewarded to comply with Allah's order to kill the Americans and plunder their money wherever and whenever they find it. We also call on Muslim ulema, leaders, youths, and soldiers to launch the raid on Satan's US troops and the devil's supporters allying with them, and to displace those who are behind them so that they may learn a lesson.

Almighty Allah said: "O ye who believe, give your response to Allah and His Apostle, when He calleth you to that which will give you life. And know that Allah cometh between a man and his heart, and that it is He to whom ye shall all be gathered."

Almighty Allah, also says: "O ye who believe, what is the matter with you, that when ye are asked to go forth in the cause of Allah, ye cling so heavily to the earth! Do ye prefer the life of this world to the hereafter? But little is the comfort of this life, as compared with the hereafter. Unless ye go forth, He will punish you with a grievous penalty, and put others in your place; but Him ye would not harm in the least. For Allah hath power over all things."

Almighty Allah also says: "So lose no heart, nor fall into despair. For ye must gain mastery if ye are true in faith."

NOTES

CHAPTER 1: THE DRUG CONNECTION: AL QAEDA AND THE TALIBAN

1. CNN terrorism analyst Peter Bergen makes mention of the bin Laden brand of heroin in *Holy War, Inc.: Inside the Secret World of Osama bin Laden* (New York: Simon and Schuster, 2002), p. 225.

2. Roland Jacquard, *In the Name of Osama bin Laden: Global Terrorism and the bin Laden Brotherhood* (Durham, NC: Duke University Press, 2002), pp. 40–41.

3. Ibid.

4. Robert Young Pelton, *The World's Most Dangerous Places*, 4th ed. (New York: Harper Resource, 2000), p. 284.

5. Ibid., p. 165.

6. Paul L. Williams, *The Complete Idiot's Guide to the Crusades* (Indianapolis: Alpha Books, 2001), pp. 112–13.

7. Daniel Benjamin and Steven Simon, *The Age of Sacred Terror* (New York: Random House, 2002), pp. 136–37.

8. Ibid.

9. Jacquard, *In the Name of Osama*, p. 42.

10. Pelton, *World's Most Dangerous Places*, p. 281.

11. Jacquard, *In the Name of Osama*, pp. 42–43.

12. Ibid., p. 38.

13. Ibid., pp. 22–23.

14. Ibid.

15. Jack Kelley, "Tribal Leaders Giving 'Our Muslim Brothers' Safe Haven," *USA Today*, January 24, 2002.

16. Yossef Bodansky, *Bin Laden: The Man Who Declared War on America* (New York: Forum, 2001), p. 315.

17. "Usama bin Laden," *FBI Ten Most Wanted Fugitives*, http://www.fbi .gov/mostwant/topten/fugitives/laden.htm (accessed April 1, 2004).

18. Testimony of L'Hossaine Kherchtou, *The United States v. Osama bin Laden et alia*, United States District Court, Southern District of New York, February 21, 2001.

19. Bergen, *Holy War, Inc.*, p. 105.

20. Ibid.

21. *The United States v. Osama bin Laden et alia*, February 14, 2001. See also Benjamin and Simon, *Age of Sacred Terror*, pp. 128–29.

22. Jason Burke, "Afghanistan: Heroin in the Holy War," *Observer* (New Delhi), December 6, 1998.

23. Fareed Zakaria, "The New Rules of Engagement," *Newsweek*, December 6, 2001.

24. US Department of Health and Human Services, "National Household Survey on Drug Abuse," *SAMHSA (Substance Abuse and Mental Health Services Administration) Office of Applied Studies*, http:// www.oas.samhsa.gov/nhsda.htm#NHSDAinfo (accessed April 1, 2004).

25. Kakharov's remarks reported in the *Washington Post*, September 7, 2001.

26. Paul L. Williams, *Al Qaeda: Brotherhood of Terror* (New York: Alpha Books, 2002), p. 165.

27. Ibid., p. 166. See also Claire Sterling, *Octopus: How the Long Reach of the Sicilian Mafia Controls the Global Narcotics Trade* (New York: Simon and Schuster, 1996), p. 162.

28. Sterling, *Octopus*, p. 162.

29. Jacquard, *In the Name of Osama*, p. 137.

30. Rachel Ehrenfeld, quoted in James Rosen's "Drug Trade Filled Coffers of Taliban, bin Laden Group," *Minneapolis Star Tribune*, September 30, 2001.

31. Simon Reeve, *The New Jackals: Ramzi Yousef, Osama bin Laden, and the Future of Terrorism* (Chicago: Northeastern University Press, 1999), p. 208.

CHAPTER 2: THE NUCLEAR SUITCASES

1. The account of Boris and Alexy comes from my contact with them from 1997 to 2000 as a consultant for the FBI.

2. Rik Luytjes is the subject of Berkeley Rice's *Trafficking: The Boom and Bust of the Air American Cocaine Ring* (New York: Simon and Schuster, 1990).

3. Marie Calvin, "Holy War with U.S. in His Sights," *Times* (London), August 16, 1998.

4. News brief, *Jerusalem Report,* October 25, 1999; "Report Links bin Laden, Nuclear Weapons," *Al-Watan al-Arabi,* November 13, 1998; Emil Torabi, "Bin Laden's Nuclear Weapons," *Muslim Magazine,* Winter 1998.

5. "Al-Majallah Obtains Serious Information on al Qaeda's Attempts to Acquire Nuclear Weapons," *Al-Majallah,* September 8, 2002.

6. "America's War on Terror: Part III: Bin Laden May Have Small Nuclear Bombs," *DEBKA*file, October 12, 2002, http://www.debka .com/article.php?aid=319 (accessed April 1, 2004). See also Robert Friedman, "The Most Dangerous Mobster in the World," *Village Voice,* May 22, 1998.

7. Brian Ross, "Portable Terror: Suitcase Nukes Raise Concern," *Primetime Thursdsay* (ABC News), November 9, 2001, http://abcnews .go.com/sections/primetime/2020/ross011108.html (accessed April 1, 2004).

8. Weldon, quoted in the *New York Post*, November 7, 1999.

9. Ibid. See also "FBI Director Admits Russians May Have Secret Weapons," *Newsmax.com*, November 8, 1999, http://www.newsmax.com/ articles/?a=1999/11/8/73601 (accessed April 1, 2004).

10. Testimony of Vasili Mitrakhin, House Committee on Government Reform, *Russian Threats to U.S. Security in Post–Cold War Era: Hearing before the Committee on Government Reform*, 106th Cong., 6th sess., January 4, 2000.

11. Testimony of Col. Stanislav Lunev, House Committee, *Russian Threats*. Lunev elaborates on the buried nukes in his book, *Through the Eyes of the Enemy* (New York: Brassey's, 2002).

12. "Feds Look for Smuggled Nukes in the United States," United Press International, *Newsmax.com*, December 21, 2001, http:// www.newsmax .com/archives/articles/2001/12/20/181037.shtm (accessed April 1, 2004).

13. Ibid.

14. Ross, "Portable Terror."

15. Ibid.

16. Testimony of Colonel Lunev, House Committee, *Russian Threats*.

17. Robert Young Pelton, *The World's Most Dangerous Places*, 4th ed. (New York: Harper Resource, 2000), p. 783.

18. Ibid.

19. Steve Goldstein, "Nukes on the Loose: The Black Market in Weapons Components," *Philadelphia Inquirer*, January 10, 1999.

20. Andrew Cockburn and Leslie Cockburn, *One Point Safe* (New York: Doubleday, 1997), pp. 101–103.

21. News brief, *Jerusalem Report*, October 25, 1999.

22. Scott Parish, "Are Suitcase Nukes on the Loose? The Story behind the Controversy," Center for Nonproliferation Studies, Monterey Institute of International Studies, Monterey, CA, November 1997.

23. Ibid.

24. Ibid.

25. "Suitcase Nukes: A Reassessment," Center for Nonproliferation Studies, Monterey Institute of International Studies, Monterey, CA, September 23, 2002.

26. Carey Sublette, "Are Suitcase Bombs Possible?" *Nuclear Weapons Archive*, May 18, 2002.

27. Ibid.

28. Yossef Bodansky, quoted in "Bin Laden Has 20 Nuclear Bombs," *World Tribune* (Washington, DC), August 9, 1999.

29. "Bin Laden Endorses 'The Nuclear Bomb of Islam,'" *Fact Sheet: The Charges against Osama bin Laden*, US Department of State, December 15, 1999, http://usinfo.state.gov/topical/pol/terror/99129502 .htm (accessed April 1, 2004).

30. "Interview with bin Laden," *Time*, December 23, 1998.

31. John Miller's interview with Osama bin Laden, ABCNews.com, May 24, 1998, http://abcnews.go.com/sections/world/DailyNews/Miller_bin laden_980609.html (accessed April 1, 2004).

32. Hamid Mir, "If US Uses Nuclear Weapons, It Will Receive Same Response," interview with Osama bin Laden, *Dawn* (Pakistan), November 10, 2001. The interview was carried by United Press International in a wire story entitled "Are bin Laden and Saddam in Nuclear Tune?" *DEBKA*file, November 10, 2001, http:// www.debka.com/article.php?aid =120 (accessed April 1, 2004). See also Evan Thomas, "The Possible Endgame and the Future of al Qaeda," *Newsweek*, November 26, 2001.

CHAPTER 3: FATWAS, FUMBLES, AND FAILURES

1. Peter L. Bergen, *Holy War, Inc.: Inside the Secret World of Osama bin Laden* (New York: Simon and Schuster, 2002), p. 97.

2. Ibid., p. 21.

3. Jane Corbin, *Al Qaeda: In Search of the Network That Threatens the World* (New York: Thunder's Mouth Press/Nation Books, 2003), p. 66.

4. Bin Laden, quoted in Bergen, *Holy War, Inc.*, p. 19.

5. *Patterns of Global Terrorism*, report by the US Department of State, 1999. See also *The United States v. Osama bin Laden et alia*, pp. 6–7.

6. *Fact Sheet: The Charges against Osama bin Laden,* US Department of State, December 15, 1999, http://usinfo.state.gov/topical/ pol/ terror/99129502.htm (accessed April 1, 2004).

7. "Jihad against Jews and Crusaders," World Islamic Front statement, February 23, 1998, in Yonah Alexander and Michael S. Swetnam, eds., *Usama bin Laden's al Qaeda: Profile of a Terrorist Network* (Ardsley, NY: Transnational Publishers, 2001).

8. Ibid.

9. Michael Grunwald, "CIA Helps Thwart Bomb Plot against Embassy in Uganda," *Seattle Times*, September 25, 1998.

10. Rohan Gunaratna, *Inside al Qaeda: Global Network of Terror* (New York: Berkley Books, 2002), p. 63.

11. President Clinton, quoted in Bergen, *Holy War, Inc.*, p. 122.

12. Bergen, *Holy War, Inc.*, p. 125.

13. Ibid.

14. Statement of *Gama'a Islamiya* in Roland Jacquard, *In the Name of Osama bin Laden: Global Terrorism and the bin Laden Brotherhood* (Durham, NC: Duke University Press, 2002), pp. 182–83.

15. Yossef Bodansky, *Bin Laden: The Man Who Declared War on America* (New York: Forum, 1999), pp. 284–85.

16. Ibid., p. 295.

17. Al-Turabi, quoted in ibid, p. 297.

18. Bergen, *Holy War, Inc.*, p. 166.

19. Ibid., p. 167.

20. Tim Weiner, "Terror Suspect Said to Anger Afghan Hosts," *New York Times*, March 4, 1999.

21. William C. Rempel, "Saudi Tells of Deal to Arrest Terror Suspects: Afghans Back-Pedaled on Hand-Over of bin Laden after U.S. Embassy Blasts," *Los Angeles Times,* August 8, 1999. See also Bodansky, *Bin Laden*, p. 282.

22. Jack Kelley, "Al Qaeda Regroups in Pakistan's No-Man's Land; Tribal Leaders Giving 'Our Muslim Brothers' Safe Haven," *USA Today,* June 24, 2002. Mullah Omar quoted in Bergen, *Holy War, Inc.*, p. 91.

23. Prince Turki, quoted in Corbin, *Al Qaeda*, pp. 69–70.

24. Larry Goodson, quoted in Ed Warner's "Taliban and al Qaeda at Odds before 1998 Bombing," *Voice of America,* August 7, 2002, http://www.why-war.com/news/2002/08/07/talibana.html (accessed April 1, 2004).

25. Matthew Levitt, "The Network of Terrorist Financing," *Washington Institute,* August 15, 2002.

26. Steve Miller, "Oregon Group Thrives Despite al Qaeda Ties," *Washington Times,* September 3, 2003.

27. Kimberly McCloud and Matthew Osborne, "WMD Terrorism and bin Laden," Center for Nonproliferation Studies, Monterey Institute of International Studies, Monterey, CA, March 7, 2001.

28. Benjamin Weiser, "U.S. Says bin Laden Aide Tried to Get Nuclear Weapons," *New York Times*, September 26, 1998.

29. Corbin, *Al Qaeda*, p. 92.

30. Bodansky, *Bin Laden*, pp. 326–27.

31. Ibid.

32. Ibid., p. 327.

33. "Bin Laden: A Nuclear Threat," EERI Daily Intelligence Report, November 7, 2001, http://www.emergencycom/2001. See also Daniel Benjamin and Steven Simon, *The Age of Sacred Terror* (New York: Random House, 2002), pp. 146–47.

34. "U.S. Operations Concentrate around Kandahar, Tora Bora," CNN, November 27, 2001.

35. Corbin, *Al Qaeda*, p. 95.

36. "Taliban Leaders Seek Official Recognition," *Times* (London), February 6, 2001.

37. Corbin, *Al Qaeda*, p. 254.

CHAPTER 4: PRESTO: WORLD WAR III

1. Daniel Benjamin and Steven Simon, *The Age of Sacred Terror* (New York: Random House, 2002), p. 37.

2. Daniel Pipes, *Militant Islam Reaches America* (New York: W. W. Norton, 2002), p. 247.

3. Jane Corbin, *Al Qaeda: In Search of the Terror Network That Threatens the World* (New York: Thunder Mouth's Press/Nation Books, 2003), p. 255.

4. Ibid., pp. 255–56.

5. Ibid., p. 257.

6. "Presidential Address to the Nation," October 7, 2001, White House Press Service, Washington, DC.

7. "Bush and Putin in Nuclear Tit-for-Tat Accord," *DEBKA*file, October 5, 2001, http://www.debka.com/article.php?aid=111 (accessed April 1, 2004).

8. Ibid.

9. "Infinite Justice, Out—Enduring Freedom, In," *BBC News*, September 25, 2001, http://news.bbc.co.uk/1/hi/world/americas/1563722.stm (accessed April 1, 2004).

10. Ibid.

11. Rohan Gunaratna, *Inside al Qaeda: Global Network of Terror* (New York: Berkley Books, 2002), p. 102.

12. Roland Jacquard, *In the Name of Osama bin Laden: Global Terrorism and the bin Laden Brotherhood* (Durham, NC: Duke University Press, 2003), p. 100.

13. Corbin, *Al Qaeda*, p. 258.

14. Peter L. Bergen, *Holy War, Inc.: Inside the Secret World of Osama bin Laden* (New York: Simon and Schuster, 2002), p. 231.

15. Luke Harding and Jason Burke, "U.S. Blamed for 100 Missile Deaths," *Guardian* (Islamabad), October 12, 2001.

16. Paul L. Williams, *Al Qaeda: Brotherhood of Terror* (Indianapolis: Alpha Books, 2002), p. 12.

17. Bin Laden, quoted in Corbin, *Al Qaeda*, p. 260.

18. Ibid.

19. Kathy Gannon, "Plans Reveal al Qaeda's Nuclear Goals," *Tulsa World*, November 16, 2001. See also, "Al Qaeda's Nuclear Plans Confirmed," *BBC News*, November 16, 2001, http://news.bbc.co.uk/1/hi/world/south_asia/1657901.stm (accessed April 1, 2004).

20. During the first week of the Afghan offensive, Master Sergeant Evander Earl Andrews was killed in a heavy equipment accident. The accident occurred in the Arabian Peninsula. Although Andrews was not killed in combat, he is often listed as the first casualty of Operation Enduring Freedom.

21. Bin Laden, quoted in Corbin, *Al Qaeda*, p. 265.

22. Richard Lloyd Parry, "Al Qaeda's Almost Immune from Attack," *Independent* (London), November 27, 2001.

23. Ibid.

24. Ibid.

25. Ibid.

26. Corbin, *Al Qaeda*, p. 267.

27. "Bin Laden 'Heard' in Tora Bora," *BBC News*, December 16, 2001, http://news.bbc.co.uk/1/hi/world/south_asia/1713307.stm (accessed April 1, 2004).

28. Antoine Blua, "Al Qaeda Fighters Routed from Tora Bora,"

Radio Free Europe, December 11, 2001, http://www.rfel.org/features/
2001/12/11122001082737.asp (accessed April 1, 2004).

29. General Myers quoted in Mark Barker's "Anti-Taliban Troops Launch Offensive on Tora Bora," *Radio Free Europe*, December 10, 2001, http://www.rferl.org/features/2001/12/10122001075819.asp (accessed April 1, 2004).

30. "Bin Laden Men to Surrender," *BBC News*, December 11, 2001, http://news.bbc.co.uk/1/hi/world/south_asia/1702200.stm (accessed April 1, 2004).

31. David Ensor, "Close In on Al Qaeda," CNN, December 21, 2001.

32. Ibid.

33. Ibid.

34. Corbin, *Al Qaeda*, p. 270.

35. Ibid.

36. Pir Baksh Bardiwal, quoted in ibid.

37. Bin Laden, text of speech in the *Washington Post*, December 27, 2001.

38. "Al Qaeda's Nuclear Plans Confirmed."

CHAPTER 5: THE MYSTERY OF SHAH-I-KOT

1. Rudyard Kipling, quoted in Jane Corbin, *Al Qaeda: In Search of the Terror Network That Threatens the World* (New York: Thunder's Mouth Press/Nation Books, 2002), p. 14.

2. Ibid., p. 15.

3. Robert Young Pelton, *The World's Most Dangerous Places,* 4th ed. (New York: Harper Resource, 2000), p. 281.

4. Ibid.

5. Bin Laden, quoted in Corbin, *Al Qaeda*, p. 21.

6. Global Intelligence Company, "Operation Anaconda: Questionable Outcomes for the United States," March 11, 2002, http://www.stratfor.com/fib/fib_view.php?ID=203443 (accessed April 1, 2004).

7. Corbin, *Al Qaeda*, p. 293.

8. Global Intelligence, "Operation Anaconda."

9. Corbin, *Al Qaeda*, p. 294.

10. John F. Burns, "U.S. Planes Pound Enemy as Troops Face Tough Fight," *New York Times,* March 4, 2002.

11. "Military Officers Criticize Rush to Use Ground Troops," *Washington Times*, March 7, 2002.

12. Ibid.

13. "U.S. Army 'On Top' in Afghan War," *Guardian* (Islamabad), March 6, 2002.

14. Ibid.

15. Ibid. See also, Corbin, *Al Qaeda*, p. 299.

16. Barry Bearak, "Details of Victory Are Unclear, but It Is Celebrated, Nonetheless," *New York Times,* March 14, 2002.

17. President Bush, quoted in Mushahid Hussein, "Operation Anaconda: Win-Win, Lose-Lose," *Asia Times*, March 22, 2002.

18. Corbin, *Al Qaeda*, pp. 298–99.

19. "U.S. Ends Operation Anaconda," *Online NewsHour*, March 18, 2002, http://www.pbs.org/newshour/updates/afghan_3-18-02.html (accessed April 1, 2004).

20. "Operation Anaconda Ends in Eastern Afghanistan," *CNN.com*, March 19, 2002, http:// www.cnn.com/2002/WORLD/asiapcf/central/03/19/ret.afghanistan.anaconda/index.html (accessed April 1, 2004).

21. Corbin, *Al Qaeda*, p. 299.

22. Vivienne Walt, "No Bodies Where Battle Began," *USA Today,* March 14, 2002.

23. Bearak, "Details of Victory."

24. Julian Borger and Richard Norton-Taylor, "U.S. Blunder Let bin Laden Escape," *Guardian* (Islamabad), April 18, 2002.

25. Sean Rayment, "Marines' Chief Under Fire for Afghan Farce," *Daily Telegraph* (Sydney), May 19, 2002.

26. Corbin, *Al Qaeda*, p. 304.

27. "Tough Namesake for Royal Marine Mission," *BBC News*, April 17, 2002, http://news.bbc.co.uk/1/hi/uk/1934613.stm (accessed April 1, 2004).

28. Rayment, "Marines' Chief Under Fire.

29. "Marines End Valley Mission," *BBC News*, April 18, 2002, http://news.bbc.co.uk/1/hi/english/world/south_asia/newsid_1936000/1936658.stm (accessed April 1, 2004).

30. Rayment, "Marines' Chief Under Fire."

31. Corbin, *Al Qaeda*, p. 306.

32. David Blair, "How the Marines Found Operation Snipe Could Not Fly," *Daily Telegraph* (Sydney), July 17, 2002.

33. James Gordon Meek, "Officials Fear al Qaeda Nuke Attack," *New York Daily News*, March 14, 2003.

34. Bill Gertz, "Al Qaeda Pursued a 'Dirty Bomb,'" *Washington Times*, October 17, 2003.

35. Ibid.

36. Ibid.

37. Ibid.

CHAPTER 6: IN THE BELLY OF THE BEAST

1. Jim Lobe, "Arms: Mercenaries Are Becoming Big Business," International Press Service, November 7, 1997.

2. Ibid.

3. Robert Young Pelton, *The World's Most Dangerous Places,* 4th ed. (New York: Harper Resource, 2000), pp. 53–54.

4. Nizam-ud din Shamzai, for instance, declared that the spilling of American blood is permissible for any reason. See ibid., p. 736.

5. Ibid., p. 745.

6. The fact that Kasmir Khan serves as bin Laden's protector has been affirmed by Pepe Escobar's "Osama Is in Kunar but U.S. Can't Get Him," *Asia Times,* August 29, 2002.

7. Jack Kelley, "Al Qaeda Regroups in Pakistan's No-Man's Land: Tribal Leaders Giving 'Our Muslim Brothers' Safe Haven," *USA Today,* June 24, 2002.

8. Ibid.

9. This observation is support by Robert D. Kaplan in his article "The Taliban," *Atlantic Monthly*, September 1, 2000.

10. Bernard Lewis, *The Political Language of Islam* (Chicago: University of Chicago Press, 1991), p. 73.

11. "Al Qaeda Is Replicating, Rejuvenating and Reorganizing," *Straits Times* (Singapore), September 16, 2003. See also Escobar, "Osama Is in Kunar."

12. Escobar, "Osama Is in Kunar."

13. Ibid.

14. "How Osama Fools Bounty Hunters," *Afghan News (Maktab Al-Jihad)*, April 9, 2003.

15. The bonds of *milmastia* among Muslims in Pakistan was verified by Tim McGirk, "In These Remote Hills, a Resurgent Al-Qaeda," *Time*, September 22, 2003.

16. Phil Zabriski, "Undefeated," *Time*, July 21, 2003.

17. Sami Yousafzai and Michael Hirsh, "The Harder Hunt for bin Laden," *Newsweek*, January 5, 2004.

CHAPTER 7: THE UNION OF RADICAL ISLAM

1. Isabel Hilton, "The Pashtun Code," *New Yorker*, December 3, 2001.

2. Robert Young Pelton, *The World's Most Dangerous Places*, 4th ed. (New York: Harper Resource, 2000), p. 300.

3. "Islamic Militants and Musharraf," *Intelligence Digest*, June 19, 2003. See also "Is Pakistan Likely to Become a Taliban State?" *Wideangle*, PBS, June 26, 2003.

4. Peter L. Bergin, *Holy War, Inc.: Inside the Secret World of Osama bin Laden* (New York: Simon and Schuster, 2002), p. 72.

5. Graham Fuller, quoted in ibid., p. 77.

6. James Meek and Ewan MacAskill, "Bonn Meeting Is Crucial, Says Alliance Leader," *Guardian* (Islamabad), November 11, 2001.

7. Gulbuddin Hekmatyar, "Call for Holy War," Afghan Islamic Press News Agency (Peshawar), January 8, 2003.

8. Scott Baldauf, "Al Qaeda Massing for New Fight," *Christian Science Monitor*, August 9, 2002.

9. Ibid.

10. "World Press Update," *Daily Times* (Islamabad), February 10, 2003, p. 2.

11. Elizabeth Neuffer, "Al Qaeda Courting Warlord, Officials Say," *Boston Globe*, July 4, 2002.

12. Daniel Benjamin and Steven Simon, *The Age of Sacred Terror* (New York: Random House, 2002), p. 393.

13. Deb Richmann, "Bush Wants $87 Billion for War on Terror," Associated Press, September 8, 2003.

14. Bureau of the Public Debt, October 3, 2003, http://www.publicdebt.treas.gov.

15. Benjamin and Simon, *Age of Sacred Terror*, p. 393.

16. Bin Laden's statement in Rohan Gunaratna's *Inside al Qaeda: Global Network of Terror* (New York: Berkley Books, 2002), pp. 300–301.

17. Bergen, *Holy War, Inc.*, p. 107.

18. Ibid.

19. Ibid.

20. Roland Jacquard, *In the Name of Osama bin Laden* (Durham, NC: Duke University Press, 2002), p. 142.

21. "Are bin Laden and Saddam in Nuclear Tune?" *DEBKA*file, November 10, 2001, http://www.debka.com/article.php?aid=120 (accessed April 1, 2004).

22. Jacquard, *In the Name of Osama*, p. 144.

23. "The Nth Country Experiment," CIA report UCRL-50248, *National Security Archive*, Washington, DC.

24. Graham Allison, "Could Worse Be Yet to Come?" *Economist*, November 1, 2001.

25. Ibid.

26. Bill Keller, "Nuclear Nightmares," *New York Times Magazine*, May 26, 2002.

27. Ibid.

28. Reuters, "Major Attacks in Afghanistan Since 2002," August 19, 2003, http://uktop100.reuters.com/latest/Police/top10/20030819-AFGHAN -ATTACKS-CHRONOLOGY.ASP (accessed April 1, 2004).

29. Olag Artyukov, "Islam's Reply to the West: 'We Cannot Openly Resist, So We Will Kill You in Your Churches,'" *Pravda*, March 18, 2002.

30. "Al Qaeda Tape: More Attacks Planned," *CNN.com*, June 24, 2002, http://www.cnn.com/2002/WORLD/meast/06/23/qatar.alqaeda.statement/?related (accessed April 1, 2004).

31. Arman Sabur and S. Roza Hassan, "Suicide Bombing Leaves 14 Dead," *Dawn*, May 9, 2002. See also "Al Qaeda Suspected in Karachi Bombing," *Newsmax.com*, June 15, 2002, http:// www.newsmax.com/archives/articles/2002/6/14/19142.shtml (accessed April 1, 2004).

32. Chris Burns, "Radical Killers behind Karachi Bomb Explosives," *CNN.com*, June 14, 2002, http://www.com/2002/WORLD/asiapcf/south/ 06/14/Karachi.blast (accessed April 1, 2004).

33. Reuters, "Major Attacks in Afghanistan Since 2002."

34. "Afghan TV: Kabul Explosives Kill 26," *CNN.com*, September 5, 2002, http://www.cnn.com/2002/WORLD/asiapcf/central/09/05/afghan.blast/ index.html (accessed April 1, 2004).

35. John Aglionby, "Double Philippine Strike Leaves Six Dead," *Guardian* (Islamabad), October 18, 2002.

36. Mitch Frank, "Timeline of Terror," *Time*, October 20, 2002.

37. Ibid.

38. Ibid.; Maria Ressa, "Extremists Blamed for Philippine Blasts," *CNN.com*, October 17, 2002, http://www.cnn.com/2002/WORLD/asiapcf/southeast/10/17/philippines.bomb/index.html (accessed April 1, 2004).

39. Reuters, "Key Attacks Linked to al Qaeda Since 9-11," November 27, 2003.

40. Frank, "Timeline of Terror."

41. Ibid.

42. George Tenet, quoted in "Two Die in Manila Bus Blast," *CNN.com*, October 18, 2002, http://www.cnn.com/2002/WORLD/asiapcf/southeast/10/18/manila.explosion/index.html (accessed April 1, 2004).

43. "Israeli Report Links Kenya Terrorists to al Qaeda," *CNN.com*, November 29, 2002, http://www.cnn.com/2002/WORLD/africa/11/28/kenya.israel/index.html (accessed April 1, 2004).

44. Steven Simon, quoted in Louis Mailer, "Terror Groups More

Decentralized, Attacked More Muslims in Home Countries amid Global Crackdown," Associated Press, December 23, 2003.

45. "Ricin Raid Slay Suspect Faces Judge,"*CBSNews.com*, January 17, 2003, http://www.cbsnews.com/stories/2003/01/07/attack/main53553.shtml (accessed April 1, 2004).

46. Ayaz Ahmed Khan, "Pipelines Destroyed in Sui," *Dawn*, January 21, 2003.

47. Leon Harris and Charles Feldman, "Ambush Attack on Americans in Kuwait," CNN, January 21, 2003.

48. B. Raman, "Al Qaeda and Taliban Target Hazaras," South Asia Analysis Group, paper 731, September 7, 2003, http:// www.saag.org/papers8/ paper731.html (accessed April 1, 2004).

49. Ayaz Gull, "Attack outside U.S. Embassy Kills at Least Two," *Voice of America*, February 28, 2003.

50. Jewel F. Candy, Carolyn O. Aiguilles, and Annette Parreno, "Bomb Explodes in Davao Airport Waiting Shed: 20 Killed, 146 Wounded," *Mina News* (Davao City, Phillipines), March 4, 2003.

51. "16 Killed in Philippine Blast," *St. Petersburg Times* (FL), April 3, 2003.

52. Rosemarie Francisco, "Thirteen Are Killed in Philippines," Reuters, May 10, 2003.

53. "Riyadh Bomb Suspect in Custody," *CBSNews.com*, June 26, 2003, http:// www.cbsnews.com/stories/2003/07/03/world/main561587.shtml (accessed April 1, 2004).

54. Ibid.

55. Associated Press, "List of Attacks in Kabul," *Newsday.com*, http://www.newsday.com/news/nationworld/wire/sns-ap-afghan-explosion-glance,0,1061769.story?coll=sns-ap-nationworld-headlines (accessed April 1, 2004).

56. Raman, "Al Qaeda and Taliban Target Hazaras."

57. Reuters, "Key Attacks Linked to Al Qaeda."

58. "Taliban Guns Down Pro-Government Cleric," *Middle East Times*, July 30, 2003.

59. Frank, "Timeline of Terror."

60. "7 Killed in Ambush in Afghanistan," *Asian Political News*, August 11, 2003.

61. "Bus Blast Kills 15 in Afghanistan," *CBSNews.com*, August 13, 2003, http://www.cbs.com/stories/2003/08/18/world/main568894.shtml (accessed April 1, 2004).

62. "Taliban in Deadly Afghan Attacks," *CBSNews.com*, August 18, 2003, http://www.cbsnews.com/stories/2003/08/22/attack/main569641 .shtml (accessed April 1, 2004).

63. Center for Defense Information, October 22, 2003, http://www .cdi.org.

64. Raman, "Al Qaeda and Taliban Target Hazaras."

65. Bin Laden, quoted in "Al Qaeda Bomb Threat to Australia," *The Age*, November 17, 2003.

66. Reuters, "Key Attacks Linked to al Qaeda."

67. Ibid.

68. Louis Mailer, "Terror Groups More Decentralized."

69. Douglas Jehl, "Al Qaeda Links Seen in Attacks on Top Saudi Security Officials," *New York Times*, December 30, 2003.

70. Center for Defense Information, December 19, 2003, http://www.cdi.org.

71. Roger Hardy, "Analysis: 'Hard Slog' against al Qaeda," *BBC News*, December 24, 2003, http://news.bbc.co.uk/1/hi/world/middle_ east/3333507.stm (accessed April 1, 2004).

72. Sam Zubeiri, "Al Qaeda Suspected after New Car Attack," *Courier-Mail* (Singapore), December 27, 2003.

73. Arnaud de Borchgrave, "So Many Fingers on the Trigger," *Washington Times*, December 30, 2003.

74. "Al Qaeda Builds a Euro Army," *Debka*, March 15, 2004.

75. Ibid.

76. Ibid.

77. Elizabeth Nash, "Madrid Atrocities: Islamic Fundamentalists or Eta," *Independent* (UK), March 12, 2004.

78. "Bin Laden Orchestrated Madrid Attacks in Person," *Debka*, March 20, 2004.

79. Ibid.

80. "Who's Next after Madrid?" *Debka*, March 13, 2004.

81. Ibid.

82. Isambard Wilkinson, "History Points Finger at Revenger for Lost Moor Kingdom," *Daily Telegraph* (UK), March 13, 2004.

83. "Who's Next after Madrid?"

84. Ibid.

85. Ibid.

86. Paul L. Williams, *The Complete Idiot's Guide to the Crusades* (Indianapolis: Alpha Books, 2001), p. 149.

87. Benjamin and Simon, *Age of Sacred Terror*, p. 127.

88. Ibid.

89. B. Raman, "Al Qaeda and Taliban Target Hazaras."

90. Benjamin and Simon, *Age of Sacred Terror*, pp. 127–28.

91. Alu Akbar Dareni, "Women's Rights Spark Controversy in Iran," Associated Press, August 4, 2002.

92. Aamir Latif, "Al Qaeda Said to Have Migrated to Iran," *Washington Times*, July 20, 2003.

93. Faye Bowers, "Iran Holds Top al Qaeda Leaders," *Christian Science Monitor*, July 28, 2003.

94. Ilene R. Prusher and Philip Smucker, "Al Qaeda Quietly Slipping into Iran, Pakistan," *Christian Science Monitor*, January 14, 2002.

95. "Al Qaeda Ordered Saudi Bombing from Iran," *Christian Science Monitor*, November 23, 2003.

96. "Iran Admits Holding al Qaeda Operatives," *CNN.com*, May 25, 2003, http://www.cnn.com/2003/WORLD/meast/05/22/alqaeda.iran (accessed April 1, 2004).

97. Ibid.

98. Joe Trento, "Pakistan and Iran's Scary Alliance," *Public Education Center*, National Security and National Resources News Services, August 15, 2003, http://www.publicedcenter.org/stories/trento/2003-08-15 (accessed April 1, 2004).

99. Ibid.

100. John M. Curtis, "Pakistan's Bomb Maker," *OnlineColumnist.com*, January 5, 2003, http://www.onlinecolomnist.com/01503.htm (accessed April 1, 2004).

CHAPTER 8: DR. STRANGELOVE

1. Bernard-Henri Levy, "Pakistan Must Provide Proof of Reforming the ISI," *South Asia Tribune*, September 14, 2003.

2. Rajesh Kumar Mishra, "Pakistan as a Proliferator State: Blame It On Dr. A. Q. Khan," South Asia Analysis Group, paper 567, December 20, 2002, http://www.saag.org/papers6/paper567.html (accessed April 1, 2004).

3. Rajesh Kumar Mishra, "Nuclear Scientific Community of Pakistan: Clear and Present Danger to Nonproliferation," South Asia Analysis Group, paper 601, July 2, 2003, http://www.saag.or/papers7/paper601.html (accessed April 1, 2004).

4. Robert J. Einhorn quoted by John M. Curtis, "Pakistan's Bomb Maker," *OnlineColuminst.com*, January 5, 2003, http://www.online columnist.com/0153.html (accessed April 1, 2004).

5. Mishra, "Pakistan as a Proliferator State."

6. John J. Curtis, "Pakistan's Bomb Maker, *Online Columnist.com*, January 5, 2003, http://www.onlinecolomnist.com/01503.htm (accessed April 1, 2004).

7. "Profile: Abdul Qadeer Khan," *BBC News*, December 20, 2003, http://news.bbc.co.uk/1/hi/world/south_asia/3343621.stm (accessed April 1, 2004).

8. Ibid.

9. Ibid.

10. Zaffar Abbas, "US Bans Trade with Pakistani Nuclear Lab," *Guardian* (Islamabad), April 2, 2003.

11. "Pakistan Scientist Brokered North Korea Deal," NBC News, October 18, 2002. See also Mishra, "Nuclear Scientific Community of Pakistan."

12. Curtis, "Pakistan's Bomb Maker."

13. Joe Trento, "Pakistan and Iran's Scary Alliance," *Public Education Center*, National Security and Natural Resources News Services, August 15, 2003, http://www.publicedcenter.org/stories/trento/2003-8-15 (accessed April 1, 2004).

14. John J. Curtis, "Why Iraq?" *OnlineColumnist.com*, January 28, 2003, http://www.onlinecolumnist.com/012803.html (accessed April 1, 2004).

15. Arnaud de Borchgrave, "Pakistan's Paranoid Panjandrum," *Washington Times*, January 20, 2003.

16. Ibid. See also Maggie Farley and Bob Drogan, "The Evil behind the Axis," *Los Angeles Times*, January 5, 2003.

17. Matt Kelley, "Libyan Success Exposes Bush Problem: Pakistan," *Tribune* (Scranton, PA), January 14, 2004.

18. Johanna McGreary, "Inside the A-Bomb Bazaar," *Time*, January 19, 2004.

19. Robert Oakley, quoted in ibid.

20. Ibid. See also B. Raman's "*Lashkar-e-Toiba*: Its Past, Present, and Future," Institute for Topical Studies, Chennai, India, December 25, 2000.

21. Raman, "*Lashkar-e-Toiba.*"

22. Ibid.

23. Ben Fenton and Ahmed Rashid, "US Hails Capture of bin Laden's Deputy," *Daily Telegraph* (Sydney), February 4, 2002.

24. Mishra, "Pakistan as a Proliferator State." See also Kaushik Kapisthalam, "Outside View: No Free Passes for Pakistan," *Washington Times*, December 30, 2003.

25. Peter L. Bergin, *Holy War, Inc.: Inside the Secret World of Osama bin Laden* (New York: Simon and Schuster, 2002), p. 244.

26. Peter Baker, "Pakistani Scientist Who Met bin Laden Failed Polygraphs, Renewing Suspicion," *Washington Post*, March 3, 2002.

27. Ibid.

28. Arnaud de Borchgrave, "Al Qaeda's Nuclear Agenda Verified," *Washington Times*, December 10, 2001.

29. Ibid.

30. Rifaat Hussain, quoted in Baker, "Pakistani Scientist Who Met bin Laden."

31. Ibid.

32. Ibid. See also Daniel Benjamin and Steven Simon, *The Age of Sacred Terror* (New York: Random House, 2002), pp. 203–204.

33. Julian Borger, "Pakistan's Nuclear Experts Advise bin Laden," *Guardian* (Islamabad), December 13, 2001.

34. Benjamin and Simon, *Age of Sacred Terror*, pp. 203–204.

35. Preston Mendenhall and Jim Miklaszewski, "Bin Laden Has Nuke Know-How," *MSNBC*, December 20, 2002, http://www.nci.org/01/12/21-01.htm (accessed April 1, 2004).

36. Sultan Bashiruddin Mahmood, quoted in Robert Sam Anson, "The Journalist and the Terrorist," *Vanity Fair*, August 2002.

37. Ibid.

38. Benjamin and Simon, *Age of Sacred Terror*, pp. 203–204.

39. Ibid.

40. Mendenhall and Miklaszewski, "Bin Laden Has Nuke Know-How." See also David Albright and Holly Higgins, "A Bomb for the Ummah," *Bulletin of Atomic Scientists* 59 (March/April 2003).

41. Albright and Higgins, "Bomb for the Ummah."

42. President George W. Bush, quoted in Mendenhall and Miklaszewski, "Bin Laden Has Nuke Know-How."

43. Ibid.

44. Baker, "Pakistani Scientist Who Met bin Laden."

45. Ibid.

46. Mishra, "Pakistan as a Proliferator State."

47. Ibid.

48. Borchgrave, "Al Qaeda Nuclear Agenda Verified."

49. Ibid.

50. "Al Qaeda Man Met Top Pakistani Nuclear Scientist," *Hindu* (New Delhi, India), May 13, 2003. See also Tim Burger and Tim McGirk, "Al Qaeda's Nuclear Contact," *Time,* May 12, 2003.

51. Burger and McGirk, "Al Qaeda's Nuclear Contact?"

52. Levy, "Paskistan Must Provide Proof."

53. Jane Corbin, *Al Qaeda: In Search of the Terror Network That Threatens the World* (New York: Thunder Mouth's Press/Nation Books, 2003), p. 366.

54. Julian West, "Pakistan Murder Exposes Missile Deal," *Sunday Telegraph* (Sydney), November 1, 1998.

55. Mishra, "Pakistan as a Proliferator State."

56. Ibid.

57. Nigel Hawkes, "The Nuclear Threat: Pakistan Could Lose Control of Its Nuclear Arsenal," *Times* (London), September 20, 2001.

58. Musharraf, quoted in Mishra, "Pakistan as a Proliferator State."

59. Ash-har Quraishi, "U.S. Supports Nuclear Pardon," CNN, February 5, 2004.

60. Ibid.

61. McGreary, "Inside the A-Bomb Bazaar."

62. Ibid.

63. Borchgrave, "Al Qaeda's Nuclear Agenda Verified."

64. Hawkes, "The Nuclear Threat."

65. Ibid.

66. Borchgrave, "Al Qaeda's Nuclear Agenda Verified."

67. Ibid. See also Abbas, "US Bans Trade with Pakistani Nuclear Lab."

CHAPTER 9: SLEEPING WITH THE ENEMY

1. The President's State of the Union Address, *CNN.com*, June 29, 2002, http://www.cnn.com/2002/ALLPOLITICS/01/28/sotu.transcript (accessed April 1, 2004).

2. United Press International, "U.S. Exposes al Qaeda Sleeper Cells from New York to Florida to L.A.," *Newsmax.com*, November 1, 2002, http://www.newsmax.com/archives/articles/2002/10/31/193315.shtml (accessed April 1, 2004).

3. Associated Press, "Two Extradited al Qaeda Suspects Head to U.S.," November 17, 2003, http://www.foxnews.com/story/0,2933,103244,00.html (accessed April 1, 2004).

4. Paul L. Williams, *Al Qaeda: Brotherhood of Terror* (Indianapolis: Alpha Books, 2002), p. 10.

5. Ibid.

6. *Al Qaeda Training Manual*, US Department of Justice, released on December 7, 2001, in accordance with the Freedom of Information Act.

7. Ibid.

8. Ibid.

9. Ibid.

10. Ibid.

11. Ibid.

12. Ibid.

13. Peter Waldman, "The Infiltrator: Ali Mohamed Served in the U.S. Army and bin Laden's Circle," *Wall Street Journal*, November 26, 2001.

14. Daniel Pipes, *Militant Islam Reaches America* (New York: W. W. Norton, 2003), p. 147.

15. Waldman, "The Infiltrator."

16. Tom Tarnipseed, "A Continuum of Terror—from *Mujahadeen* to al Qaeda," *Common Dreams News Center,* November 28, 2001, http://www.commondreams.org/views01/1128-10.htm (accessed April 1, 2004).

17. Ibid.

18. Waldman, "The Infiltrator."

19. Ibid.

20. Pipes, *Militant Islam*, p. 147.

21. Nabil Sharef, quoted in Waldman, "The Infiltrator."

22. Pipes, *Militant Islam*, p. 149. See also news briefs in the *Tampa Tribune*, June 10, 2001, and the *Jerusalem Post*, June 20, 2001.

23. Pipes, *Militant Islam*, p. 151. See also news briefs from the *Sydney Morning Herald,* December 10, 2001.

24. "Current Time," *Bulletin of Atomic Scientists* 42, no. 17 (March 25, 2003).

CHAPTER 10: BEHOLD A PALE HORSE

1. Peter L. Bergen, *Holy War, Inc.: Inside the Secret World of Osama bin Laden* (New York: Simon and Schuster, 2002), p. 242.

2. Ibid.

3. Paul L. Williams, *Al Qaeda: Brotherhood of Terror* (Indianapolis: Alpha Books, 2002), p. 10.

4. Igor Valynkin, quoted in "Suitcase Nukes: A Reassessment," *Research Story of the Week*, Center for Nonproliferation Studies, Monterey Institute of International Studies, Monterey, CA, September 23, 2003.

5. "Jihad against Jews and Crusaders," World Islamic Front statement, February 23, 1998, in *Usama bin Laden's al Qaeda: Profile of a Terrorist Network*, ed. Yonah Alexander and Michael S. Swetnam (Ardsley, NY: Transnational Publishers, 2001).

6. See chapter 8. Also Preston Mendenhall and Jim Miklaszewski, "Bin Laden Has Nuke Know-How," *MSNBC*, December 20, 2003, http://www.nci.org/01/12/21-01.htm (accessed April 1, 2004); David Albright and Holly Higgins, "A Bomb for the Ummah," *Bulletin of Atomic Scientists* 59 (March/April 2003); and Arnaud De Borchgrave, "Al Qaeda's Nuclear Agenda Verified," *Washington Times*, December 10, 2003.

7. "Interview with Mullah Omar," *BBC News*, November 15, 2001, http://www.bbc.co.uk/1/hi/world/south_asia/1657368.stm (accessed April 1, 2004).

8. United Press International, "U.S. Exposes al Qaeda Sleeper Cell from New York to Florida to L.A.," *Newsmax.com*, November 1, 2002, http://www.newsmax.com/archives/articles/2002/10/31/193315.shtml (accessed April 1, 2004).

9. Allison's statements included in Brian Ross, "Portable Terror: Suitcase Nukes Raise Concern," *Primetime Thursdsay* (ABC News), November 9, 2001, http://abcnews.go.com/sections/primetime/2020/ross011108.html (accessed April 1, 2004).

10. Osama Bin Laden, "Declaration of War against the Americans Occupying the Land of the Two Holy Places," August 23, 1996, in Alexander and Swetnam, *Usama Bin Laden's Al Qaeda*.

11. Sulaiman Abu Ghaith, "Why We Fight America," special dispatch 388, Middle East Media Research Institute, *MEMRI*, June 12, 2002, http://memri.org/bin/articles.cgi?Page=archives&Area=sd&ID=SP38802 (accessed April 1, 2004).

12. Ibid.

13. "Bin Laden's Search for Nuclear Weapons," *US News and World Report*, October 5, 1998.

14. Untitled article, *Jerusalem Post*, October 25, 1999; Lexi Krock and Rebecca Deusser, "Nuclear Chronology of Events, PBS, February 2000, from a broadcast transcript delivered to the FBI; Felipe Rodriquez, "Analysis: Terrorism with Weapons of Mass Destruction," Nuclear Age Peace Foundation, *WagingPeace.org*, September 17, 2001, http://www.wagingpeace.org/articles/2001/09/17_rodriquez_analysis .htm (accessed April 1, 2004); "America's War on Terror: Part III: Bin Laden May Have Small Nuclear Bombs," *DEBKA*file, October 12, 2002, http://www.debka.com/article.php?aid=319 (accessed April 1, 2004); Utman Tizgart, "Does bin Laden Really Possess Weapons of Mass Destruction? Tale of Russian Mafia Boss Semion Mogilevich, Who Supplied bin Laden with the Nuclear 'Dirty Bomb,'" *Al-Majallah*, November 25, 2001; Adam Nathan and David Leppard, "Al Qaeda's Men Held Secret Meetings to Build 'Dirty Bomb,'" *Sunday Times* (London), September 8, 2002.

15. Hamid Mir, "If US Uses Nuclear Weapons, It Will Receive Same Response," interview with Osama bin Laden, *Dawn* (Pakistan), November 10, 2001. The interview was carried by United Press International in a wire story entitled "Are bin Laden and Saddam in Nuclear Tune?" *DEBKA*file, November 10, 2001, http://www.debka.com/article.php?aid=120 (accessed April 1, 2004).

16. Richard Sale, "Israel Finds Radiological Backpack Bomb," United Press International, October 14, 2001, http://www.papillonsartpalace.com/israelf.htm (accessed April 1, 2004).

17. Richard Sale, "Feds Look for Smuggled Nukes in the United States," United Press International, *Newsmax.com*, December 21, 2001, http://www.newsmax.com/archives/articles/2001/12/20/181037.shtml (accessed April 1, 2004); see also note 1.

18. Ibid. Sale is not only a UPI correspondent but also a former CIA agent. He is recognized as one of the world's leading authorities on nuclear terrorism.

19. Robert D. McFadden, "A Nation Challenged: Tip on Nuclear Attack Risk Was Kept from New Yorkers," *New York Times*, March 4, 2002, p. 11.

20. Naveed Miraj, "Al Qaeda Nukes May Already Be in the US," *Frontier Post* (Islamabad), November 11, 2001.

21. "N-Weapons May Be in US Already," *Daily Telegraph* (Sydney), November 14, 2001. The *Telegraph* article not only substantiates Miraj's report but also provides additional information about the two nuclear suitcases that have been smuggled into the United States.

22. Sale, "Feds Look for Smuggled Nukes."

23. Ibid.

24. Barton Gellman, "Fears Prompt U.S. to Beef-Up Nuclear Terror Detection," *Washington Post*, March 3, 2002.

25. Sale, "Feds Look for Smuggled Nukes."

26. Ibid.

27. Flynn, quoted in ibid.

28. This information, supported by Israeli intelligence, is contained in *DEBKA*file, September 14, 2002, http://www.debka.com.

29. Shaykh Hisham Kabbani, "Islamic Extremism: A Viable Threat to U.S. National Security," report published by the US Department of State, January 7, 1999. See also "Dispute between Muslim Groups Goes Public," *Washington Report on Middle East Affairs*, April/May 1999; Daniel Pipes, "Naked: Muslims versus Terror," *Forward*, July 16, 1999; and Sheikh Abdul Hadi Palazzi, "The Islamists Have It Wrong," *Middle East Quarterly*, September 2001.

30. Kabbani, "Islamic Extremism."

31. Daniel Pipes, *Militant Islam Reaches America* (New York: W. W. Norton, 2003), p. 123.

32. Dave Eberhart, "Muslim Moderate Kabbani Firm on Terrorist Nuclear Threat," United Press International, *Newsmax.com*, November 19, 2001, http://www.newsmax.com/archives/articles/2001/11/16/172201 .shmtl (accessed April 1, 2004).

33. "Al-Qaida's Favorite October Target Dates: Military Intelligence Specialists Offer Possible Imminent Terror Scenarios," *WorldNetDaily*, September 30, 2002, http://www.worldnetdaily.com/news/article.asp ?ARTICLE _ID=29100 (accessed April 1, 2004).

34. Paul L. Williams, *The Complete Idiot's Guide to the Crusades* (Indianapolis: Alpha Books, 2001), p. xxi.

35. Ambassador Thomas Graham Jr., quoted in Stuart Taylor Jr., "A Nuclear Nightmare: It Could Happen Today," *Atlantic*, November 14, 2001.

CHAPTER 11: WHAT WILL HAPPEN

1. John McPhee, *The Curve of Binding Energy* (New York: Farrar, Strauss and Giroux, 1973), p. 225.
2. Ibid., p. 226.
3. Ibid.
4. Council on Foreign Relations, "Terrorism: Questions and Answers," 2002, http://cfrterrorism.org.
5. Roland Watson, "The Destructive Effects of a Nuclear Suitcase Bomb," Center for Libertarian Studies, *LewRockwell.com*, January 4, 2002, http://www.lewrockwell.com/watson/watson27.htm (accessed April 1, 2004). Mr. Watson is a correspondent for the *Times* (London).
6. Ibid.
7. Ibid.
8. Ibid.
9. Graham Allison, "The Causes of the 9-11 Attacks and the Scope of the Threats," *World Media Association*, February 20, 2003, http://www.wmassociation.com/reports/spkers/allison.html (accessed April 1, 2004). Mr. Allison is the director of Harvard University's Belfer Center for Science and International Studies.
10. Watson, "Destructive Effects."
11. Allison, "Causes of the 9-11 Attacks."
12. Watson, "Destructive Effects."
13. Bill Keller, "Nuclear Nightmares," *New York Times Magazine*, May 26, 2002.
14. Stuart Taylor Jr., "A Nuclear Nightmare: It Could Happen Today," *Atlantic*, November 14, 2001.
15. Keller, "Nuclear Nightmares."
16. Ibid.

17. Daniel Benjamin and Steven Simon, *The Age of Sacred Terror* (New York: Random House, 2002), p. 398.

18. Ibid., p. 399.

19. Josh Meyer and Greg Krikorian, "US Braces for Attacks by al Qaeda," *Los Angeles Times,* December 24, 2003.

20. Keller, "Nuclear Nightmares."

21. Saad al-Fagih, quoted in Michael Eliot, "Al Qaeda: Alive and Ticking," *Time*, October 20, 2002.

EPILOGUE

1. "Usama bin Laden," *FBI Ten Most Wanted Fugitives*, http://www.fbi.gov/mostwant/topten/fugitives/laden.htm (accessed April 1, 2004).

2. Joseph Farah, "Is bin Laden the Mahdi?" G2 Bulletin, September 8, 2003, http://wnd.com. This is a subscription site only, but excerpts from Farah's article can be found at *WorldNetDaily*, http://www.worldnetdaily.com/news/article.asp?ARTICLE_ID=34469 (accessed April 1, 2004).

3. Christopher M. Newport, "The Next Mahdi: Putting bin Laden in Historical Perspective," *Armed Forces Journal*, September 2002.

4. Farah, "Is bin Laden the Mahdi?" See also Robert Fisk, "Obsession with bin Laden Crosses All Frontiers," *Independent*, October 22, 2001.

5. "Information of the Prophesied Imam Mahdi," *Idara Dawat o-Irshad*, Alexandria, Virginia, 2002 published online at http://www.irshad.org/mission.php.

6. Ibid.

7. Ibid.

8. Farah, "Is bin Laden the Mahdi?"

INDEX